# CA$HING IN

## IN

LISA BERGER
DONELSON BERGER
C. WILLIAM EASTWOOD

# CA$HING IN

## GETTING THE MOST WHEN YOU SELL YOUR BUSINESS

**WARNER BOOKS**

A Warner Communications Company

TO

MOM AND DAD

CAPTAIN SQUIGIWIGG

MOM AND DAD

Copyright © 1988 Lisa Berger, Donelson Berger, C. William Eastwood

All rights reserved

Warners Books, Inc., 666 Fifth Avenue, New York, NY 10103

A Warner Communications Company

Printed in the United States of America

First printing: November 1988

10 9 8 7 6 5 4 3 2 1

Book Design by Nick Mazzella.

Library of Congress Cataloging-in-Publication Data

Berger, Lisa.
    Cashing in : getting the most when you sell your business / by
Lisa Berger, Donelson Berger, C. William Eastwood.
        p.  cm.
    Includes index.
    1. Business enterprises, Sale of—United States.   I. Berger,
Donelson.   II. Eastwood, C. William.   III. Title.
HD1393.25.B467   1988
    658.1′6—dc19                                          88-14909
    ISBN 0-446-51441-1                                        CIP

# CONTENTS

# CA$HING IN

# INTRODUCTION

On the first day of March 1985, Donelson Berger culminated years of work and worry and cashed in: he sold his company for millions. On Friday he was chairman and majority shareholder of a private company with hundreds of employees, and the next Monday he had a large investment portfolio and was working for someone else. It was a once-in-a-lifetime experience that was exhilarating and yet anxiety-producing.

Don is an adept negotiator who knows the ins and outs of how to make a deal—what motivates a buyer as well as what the intricacies of earn-outs and valuation formulas are. Nevertheless, negotiations stretched for more than nine months as he and the buyer wrestled over prices and terms. Every day he was on the phone, pulling numbers from accountants, plotting strategy with lawyers or bargaining with the buyer.

In a way, this book emerged from that sale. Don found that selling a company is a state of mind as well as a step-by-step process, and an owner with the right information and attitude can substantially increase the rewards. Don was convinced that sellers like himself could use a book on how to sell a company—a guide for owners of small and midsized companies who want to convert sweat into money at the best possible price and conditions.

The U.S. Congress provided another reason for this book when it passed the 1986 Tax Reform Act. Everyone knows the tremendous impact this law has had on personal taxes. For the company seller, the effect is even more dramatic.

The Tax Reform Act changed the rules of the ballgame. It phased out long-term capital gains and some antiquated doctrines of corporate tax law, sparked a revival of S Corporations and partnerships for small, privately held businesses, and lowered individual and corporate rates.

1

The Tax Reform Act altered many facets of a company sale, from whether and how a company incorporates to what kind of payment an owner wants. Some sellers feel cheated by the new law, especially by the elimination of preferential treatment on long-term capital gains. They may have spent decades building a business, hoping someday to cash in for a handsome profit with only a 20 percent tax bite. Now they feel robbed. But where the tax law taketh away, it giveth elsewhere.

The tax law has altered only how a seller will profit. There's still room for creative deal making and innovative structuring so that a seller can limit taxes and hold on to well-earned gains. This book shows where those opportunities lie so sellers can minimize taxes under the new rules.

Who are the sellers we write about? They are largely founders and owners who control or own the majority stock in a private or closely held company. They are individual entrepreneurs, second or third generation in a family-owned business, or partners with complementary talents. In size, their companies generally range from $150,000 to $70 million revenues. The firms are partnerships and sole proprietorships as well as corporations.

We have generally not talked about sellers of large companies. They're in a different league. Those companies are often publicly owned and retain high-paid acquisition experts to conduct every aspect of a sale. These people usually watch from the owner's box— they're not in the field struggling with every aspect of a sale.

We have woven throughout the book the stories of individual sellers. We identified and selected these people through business contacts, reports in mergers and acquisitions journals, and news stories. We required only that they be owners of private companies and that their companies vary in size and industry. And, of course, we needed a willingness to share the details of their sales. Their stories are just that—*their* stories. Where necessary, we verified certain information, but we generally preferred to relate the seller's version of the transaction. That, after all, is what this book is all about.

Almost all of our owners were glad they sold and pleased with the outcome. Nonetheless, in hindsight, each would have done something differently: asked for more money, altered the terms, sold earlier or later . . . something. There's no flawless sale. Their stories are not models of perfection but accounts of real experiences and the myriad things that can go right, and wrong, with a sale.

Enough about the why and how of this book. On to the more enticing question: How do you sell a company?

# CHAPTER 1

# WHY SELL?

Why sell? Lots of reasons: some owners want to retire, some want to convert equity into cash, some get ill and can't continue working, some are burned out from the worries and hassle, and some want just to do something else. But the most common motive, and the thread running through every owner's mind, is money. And the more the better.

Selling a company is about money and the best price. Sounds simple, but it isn't. Putting a price tag on a business you've devoted years to building—a price that someone will actually pay—requires more than picking a number out of the air. Everyone has a financial dream. It can be within easy reach or impossible to attain. Selling price equals the sum total of business and personal needs and expectations. It's a number woven out of your company and out of your expectations about your family life and your future. To begin to find the dollar figure of your dreams, ask yourself these questions:

- What's the minimum amount I'll settle for?
- Will I sell assets or stock? (A corporation can sell stock or assets; a sole proprietorship has no stock to sell. In this case, what assets are saleable?)
- How much risk am I willing to take? (Terms other than cash may be easier to bargain for, but carry more risk.)

- How much am I willing to pay in taxes? Where will I get the money to pay them?
- What will I do with the profit?
- What will I do after the sale?
- Do I need, financially or psychologically, a job with the new owner? (Employment contracts are common and you may be paid more, or less, than you pay yourself.)
- Do I want to stay with the company and work for a percentage of future earnings?

Your decision to sell may start with "How much?" but selling price is only part of the answer. Even though a sale produces a financial windfall, it also changes an owner's personal life and business. These carry financial implications of their own. A common metaphor for selling a company is courtship and marriage. The comparison is apt. Selling is a major plunge that can alter everything from your monthly household budget to your image as an independent entrepreneur. It's a once-in-a-lifetime experience. It's the culmination of years of work. It's the beginning of a new chapter in your life.

Let's look at the business implications first. Selling causes a major or minor reshuffle in a seller's business and personal life. How much of an upheaval depends on your preparation and what you want to accomplish. Here's what a sale can do for a company. It can:

- Create jobs and other opportunities for successors.
- Bring in management and depth for growth.
- Add working capital.
- Diversify into different business areas or product lines.
- Convert hard assets and equity into cash.
- Reduce risk of losses or diminishing profits.
- Establish new business connections and expand into different markets.
- Strengthen market share over a competitor.
- Finance extensive improvements or modernizing.
- Obtain insurance that has been unavailable or prohibitively expensive.

The decision to sell can build up slowly. It may come after months of wrestling with a problem. An owner grappling with a seemingly insoluble managerial, financial or operations dilemma finally contemplates selling as the last solution. Selling to achieve a fresh perspective and a different style of management has saved many businesses.

**ONE SELLER'S STORY: Waters Associates, Inc.**

This is what happened to Jim Waters, a proud Massachusetts engineer and physicist who devoted twenty years to creating a multimillion-dollar company. An entrepreneur and scientist, he did not easily assume the mantle of seller. For almost a year he grappled with a faltering company trying to correct a damaging management situation. He wanted to save his company, not sell it. Ultimately, the only way to rescue his enterprise was to relinquish control to another owner who would hire a new chief executive.

Jim Waters started his first company, James L. Waters, Inc., right after college. He formed his second company, Waters Associates, in the early 1960s with five employees who had worked with him before. Waters Associates designed and manufactured instruments to analyze chemical mixtures.

In the mid-1970s the industrial world discovered complex chemicals. Pharmaceutical companies were analyzing the chemicals for the Food and Drug Administration; university professors were synthesizing new compounds they wanted to identify and separate; food manufacturers were testing products for saccharin and pesticides; meat packers were examining beef for steroids; and soft-drink companies were monitoring caffeine in sodas. Demand for all sorts of chemical analyses skyrocketed. Between 1971 and 1978 Waters Associates grew 40 percent a year and topped $75 million in annual revenues.

Jim Waters's offspring grew too fast: its managers started to lose control. As a hands-off majority owner and chairman of the board, Jim gave managers the freedom to hire, fire, make decisions and commit resources. But market share slipped from 40 to 35 percent, profits dropped, research and development projects fell behind schedule, and product quality deteriorated.

Waters saw his company headed toward a danger zone. He tried all kinds of managerial remedies. He even took the unusual step of switching roles. He moved the chief executive officer away from day-to-day administration and assigned him to planning long-term strategy. He shifted the chief financial officer to operations. But the line graphs continued to point downward.

"Frank's way was all right," Waters reflects about the chief executive officer, "as long as he had good, strong people that he delegated to. Unfortunately, Frank didn't pick good, strong people. Left to their own devices, they simply didn't perform and he didn't weed the garden." Waters couldn't fire the chief executive because company ranks contained no one to take his place. For top management, Waters had to look outside.

Although Waters suspected he had made a mistake with the CEO, he still trusted his own judgment. He knew his strengths and weaknesses and rejected a move that many owners might have resorted to—stepping back in. "I'm not a manager, I'm more of a leader. Managing is not my bag, not what I'm good at. My strength is starting companies. I'm all right as a manager up to a hundred fifty people, but beyond that, management gets to be very different. It's a hard, hard job being a good manager of a large company. You don't do anything. Everybody else does things and you evaluate whether they've done them right. I tend to roll up my sleeves and get into details."

Waters decided to sell. But sellers rarely make such a decision unilaterally or in a vacuum. Even the most independent founder may need the approval of others. Spouses, family members, board members or minority shareholders usually insist on a voice. These voices act as checks and balances, testing a seller's resolve and reasoning. If a seller's rationale makes sense corporately, economically or personally, he or she can convince others.

In Jim Waters's mind, selling to a firm that could furnish strong management was the only open avenue. Nevertheless, he could not act alone. He and his family controlled 30 percent of the company stock, but the entire board of directors had final authority. For almost a year, Waters and the board had wrestled with their troubled company. He met individually with directors and shared the frustrations of putting the company on track.

At first, the board did not believe the troubles were as bad as Waters described. "The board had a problem with this wild entrepreneur suddenly saying that his company was being ruined. I could understand their point of view."

Finally, events within the company itself persuaded the board. None of the internal adjustments was yielding results. The board watched helplessly as Waters Associates' most valuable asset, dominant market share, continued to dwindle. They could overlook many shortcomings, but losing market share was tantamount to calling in the wrecking ball. The slides had to be stopped.

The day before a regular bimonthly board meeting, Waters telephoned the directors and informed them that he would be urging, and if necessary forcing, a search for a merger partner. While the board may have been surprised at Jim Waters's determination, it acquiesced.

Waters was confident of a quick sale: "It was an attractive company—I knew we'd have no problem finding a partner." Ironically, the solution to their troubles and new owner had been sitting next to them all the time. Not only was he a board member but also chief executive officer of Millipore Corporation and a close observer of the Waters Associates' management turmoil. There had even been a brief chat months earlier about Millipore buying Waters Associates, but the conversation apparently did not go beyond light speculation.

Two days after Jim Waters launched his search, the Millipore chief executive telephoned. Millipore was in a similar business— it manufactured chemical filters—and had managers who could turn Waters Associates around.

Millipore proposed taking over Waters Associates through a one-for-one stock swap. Every Waters Associates shareholder would receive a share of Millipore stock, which was trading over-the-counter for $29. Water Associates stock was publicly traded at $25 a share.

Jim Waters delivered the offer to the board with his endorsement and commitment to pledge his stock to the sale. The bid was attractive for three reasons: the $4 gain on each share of stock, the absence of tax liabilities on a stock swap and Millipore's excellent reputation.

For Jim Waters, the sale meant a $5 million personal gain on paper and nothing for the Internal Revenue Service. Of course, the securities bore restrictions. Waters was limited to how much Millipore stock he could sell and he had to adhere to insider restrictions. ("Lettered stock" such as this restricts how long someone must keep it and when and how it can be sold.)

A company sale can be bogged down by accountants and lawyers who pore over books and unearth new information that precipitates further negotiations. This is especially true for private companies where owners maintain confidential records and buyers are unfamiliar with a potential acquisition. In the Waters Associates sale, events moved smoothly because neither company was private—both were public corporations and their financial records were open to all. Also easing the sale was Millipore's status as an informed buyer.

Waters and the board voted overwhelmingly to accept the Millipore offer with the final agreement dependent on in-depth investigations ("due diligence") by both sides.

Jim Waters felt a little wistful about leaving his company but doesn't regret it. He sold the company to improve its performance. Within six months of the merger agreement, Waters Associates had new managers, and today the company is profitable and holds a 40 percent market share. And Jim Waters's Millipore stock has risen, split and risen again.

## THE RIGHT TIME

"I ran one of the great little radio stations in the country. There's no better job than running a flamboyant rock station. You can make a ton of money and do and say ANYTHING. But I did it for years and years and, you know, it was time to move on."    —Frank Wood

Timing is critical in a sale. Both you and your company have to be ready. Moving too soon or overreacting to a temporary situation can cut into hard-earned gains.

The worst reason to sell is because a buyer walks through the door. Confronted with a living, breathing buyer, sellers rush into a deal, justifying their haste with, "This is a chance in a lifetime" or "Buyers don't grow on trees." More than one buyer exists for a company worth selling. If you have one offer, others will materialize. Don't necessarily jump at the first proposal—other suitors may be out there.

Owners may be tempted to react impulsively. They may sell just to get even with a competitor or because they are tired of coping with the lows of a business cycle. All businesses hit rough spots or doldrums—times when owners doubt their determination and ability: the "Oh hell, what do I do now?" moments. This is precisely the wrong time to sell. Sell when you are strong, not weak.

Other bad reasons are impatience for quick financial rewards; unrealistic financial, business or personal goals; misjudging how a buyer intends to change the company and your role in it; and the absence of other immediate offers.

## WHAT TO SAY TO A BUYER

You will swap information with many potential buyers. The most effective strategy is to adhere to the principle, Give a little, get a little. Be interested but not overeager, sincere and forthcoming but not unguarded. When buyers ask "Why?" your answer either intrigues them or makes them hesitant. Carefully pick what you say and how you say it. Be honest and open, but don't immediately reveal everything about yourself and your company. If you're evasive, however, buyers suspect skeletons in the closet. In these early encounters, probe the buyer to find out why he or she is interested in your company.

Later on in the courtship, if sale talks get serious, both sides learn plenty about each other. Until then, don't reveal too much. You don't really know to whom you are talking. Competitors and employees posing as buyers have been known to ferret out confidential company information. At the beginning, play your cards closely until you know the buyer is sincere and can afford your company.

⌈ If a family situation, personal crisis or disastrous year is pressing you to sell, keep quiet for now.⌉(Eventually you will disclose everything relevant, but not in these opening rounds.) If your shop is collapsing behind you,⌈don't say it.⌉The panicked or desperately eager seller scares buyers. And exposing weak spots or dwelling on troublesome reasons for selling gives a buyer the upper hand. You lose negotiating chips if a buyer knows you *must* sell.

⌈Some reasons for a sale are personal: poor health of an owner or family member; personal conflict with co-owners or shareholders; debts, alimony, settlement costs; burnout or disenchantment with the business; divorce. Reveal these only if they are relevant, and even then wait until after initial discussions.⌉

Sellers worried about sale talks leaking to employees or clients should require a potential buyer to sign a nondisclosure agreement. A buyer promises not to reveal confidential information or even that the two sides have met. Buyers may also want nondisclosure agreements. They may want to keep talks secret from competitors and, if a public company, not influence stock prices.

A skilled buyer romances a seller with lots of handholding—daily phone calls, long lunches and dinners at private clubs or expensive restaurants, rounds on the golf course. In short, a business friendship develops. Friendly chemistry is important and overt antagonism can kill a deal. But friendliness can be deceptive. A seller eager for a match with an ideal buyer is easily lulled into a feeling of camaraderie and shared ambitions. In this atmosphere, you may forget that the buyer's goal may not be the same as yours. He may want you to stay on while you want a large up-front payment and a clean exit. Or vice versa: you want to remain with the company to reap a big earn-out down the road, and the buyer wants you out so he can strip your rich assets.

## ONE SELLER'S STORY: Western Wholesale and Supply Company

Fear, and the pressure of a mounting debt, forced Boyd Hill into selling Western Wholesale and Supply, his Boise, Idaho, building supply firm. A competitor was moving into his territory, a much bigger company that offered discount prices, and Boyd doubted he could survive a head-to-head contest. Convinced it was sink or sell, he assembled a sale package. While the buyer might have sensed he was trapped, Boyd marshaled all his bargaining muscle and negotiated a profitable sale.

Boise is a largely Mormon community that expands and contracts with potato crops and a few major corporations such as Ore-Ida, Morrison Knudsen and Boise Cascade. The fortunes of Western Wholesale rose and fell with the pace of farm, home and business construction.

Hill had lived through the cycles of the building trades. He knew good times and hard, and was a realist about his company's prospects. After straining to buy it in 1975 with a loan from the Small Business Administration, he forged ahead to nearly triple sales to almost $3 million. New businesses and executives were migrating into the region, and Hill's enterprise thrived. Selling roofing, shingles, Sheetrock and nails, he managed a $142,000 profit in 1978.

Then in 1979 soaring interest rates ravaged the construction industry, and Hill watched sales plunge to $1.2 million. Wrong-footed by the downturn, he found himself overstaffed, committed to truck payments and holding blueprints to a new warehouse. For the first time, Boyd Hill had to lay off people, cut salaries and abandon dreams of expansion. He also owed the bank $381,000 and was paying as much as 22 percent on part of the loans.

Slowly, the company climbed from its hole. Hill slashed expenses, starting with his own salary, then mothballed costly equipment. He pressured customers to settle accounts. In 1982 he branched into a pneumatic nail distribution line, and the following year he paid off the SBA. The rumor mill brought the next company crisis. A California building supply company, a regional outfit with sales around $400 million, was expanding into the Boise Valley. The newcomer was not only bigger than Hill, but also offered a discount on the supplies Hill stocked.

Hill resisted selling. He was fifty-three years old with eight children—he couldn't afford to retire and saw no prospects of a job if he abandoned Western Wholesale. Nevertheless, he telephoned the Salt Lake City manager of Pacific Building Products.

"I understand you're interested in moving into the Boise market," he ventured. "I'm not selling now, but if I were offered the right price I wouldn't mind having an opportunity to sit down and talk to you."

The company dispatched a regional sales manager and a division manager to Boise. Hill showed them around for ninety minutes while they talked about building supplies. He didn't volunteer financial information and told the men they could check his credit rating with Dun & Bradstreet.

Hill deftly played what few cards he had. Instead of revealing too much to these first contacts, he waited to meet the company president and decision-maker. "In the preliminary discussions I didn't feel there was enough in the business for me to sell out. And I had to have a job."

The first meeting ended on a positive note, and Hill assumed they would proceed to the next phase. But wires crossed and for three months both sides waited. Apparently, the buyer expected to hear how much Hill wanted and Hill expected to hear that the buyer was sincerely interested. Finally, an independent salesman told Hill that Pacific Building Products was definitely interested and to call them.

Lines of communication again open, the next conference solved Hill's employment worries. The buyer agreed to let him keep Paslode Products, the pneumatic nail distribution enterprise he operated under Western Wholesale's roof. "At that time I got more interested because I could see an opportunity to liquidate out of debt, take a salesman with me and build another small business."

They scheduled negotiations. The president, senior vice president, regional manager and division manager flew to Boise on the company jet and convened at the offices of Hill's attorney. Sitting with Hill was his accountant. Talks opened with the president laying down terms.

"He said they were interested in the Boise market," Hill remembers, "and would prefer to buy an existing business. But they had the resources to start one if they had to. They would pay no goodwill and buy only assets. It was a matter of determining the price of inventory and equipment. He was willing to pay net cost of inventory delivered Boise and offered used value on the equipment and supplies. I really don't know how they arrived at the values. They just made the offer of the maximum they would pay."

Hill reacted coolly. The offer on the equipment amounted to 28 percent below invoice cost. "When I bought equipment I wasn't cheap. I had a well-run business and my equipment maintained in A-1 condition. All my trucks were air brake–type systems, forklifts were air brake, everything was compatible."

Although his advisors tried to undermine his determination, Hill held his ground. "My attorney for some reason or other was afraid I would lose the sale. I felt there were several times that he didn't want to go along with asking for more for fear that I would be totally rejected and out in the cold. My accountant felt the same way. He looked at the alternatives—what would happen if I didn't sell versus selling and walking away out of debt."

An hour into the meeting Hill huddled with his lawyer and accountant and returned to the bargaining table. He accepted the offer for net cost on the inventory but rejected the offer on the equipment and supplies. The meeting broke up without an agreement.

For two weeks neither side budged. Hill agonized. "I felt a tremendous amount of pressure to sell. The ultimate decision came down to: Am I financially able to go head-to-head with a major competitor and lose some of my accounts? Would I be able to service my debt load and compete with them on price? I felt, Well, the gun's at my back. I either sell at their price or possibly be forced out of business."

At last the buyer telephoned with a counteroffer. Hill had asked $210,000 for equipment. The buyer first offered $80,000— now he came back with $150,000. Hill conceded, and they arranged to hammer out details.

The president of the California buyer did not attend closing. "He stayed away so his men could be tough, hard negotiators," Hill concludes. "That way he didn't have to be involved in discussions and maybe get talked into something he didn't want to do. They negotiated with the attitude that if this sale isn't closed by 5 p.m., they would pack their bags and go home. That was the gun at my back."

The only alteration in the terms involved office furniture and supplies. The buyer had listed them no cost, and Hill rejected the arrangement. "When it got down to hard negotiations on desks and office supplies and miscellaneous things, they didn't want to pay me the price I asked for. So I said, 'Fine, I'll keep it.' This left me well-equipped for my new business."

By sundown, Hill had sold Western Wholesale for $532,900. He immediately paid off the $381,000 bank loan. The buyer deposited the remainder into an escrow account until Hill collected his receivables. Not included in the sale was inventory worth about $200,000, a piece of land and Paslode Products. Hill signed a two-year noncompete agreement, although he received nothing in exchange, and the buyer agreed not to compete with Paslode Products.

While he wishes he had gotten something for goodwill, Hill is relieved. Selling, even with "a gun at his back," was better than being squeezed out of business.

## PLUNGING AHEAD

> "When these things [an offer to buy] happen you should be prepared. This means you have to talk with your wife, family, friends, so you can deal with it promptly and in a way that is sophisticated enough so that people know they're dealing with someone of substance."
> —Bill Janss

Selling a company is like embarking on a new career. It demands persistence and single-mindedness. You have to believe your company is saleable—it has a market value and you're prepared to cash in.

The decision can be emotional. Sellers grow attached to their creations. Some have lavished more time on their companies than on their families. Giving up their only offspring is a wrenching experience. Ego is involved, too. Sellers like running companies and taking action. They're accustomed to responsibility and having the final word. Relinquishing this role—giving up the satisfaction of making decisions—can be painful. Some never let go. Successful sellers have to shed these attachments and, at least temporarily, their images as authority figures. They have to view their company as a means to another end, not as an end in itself. The real issue for many sellers is the gut: Are you mentally prepared to sell and change your life? Most proposed business sales fall apart not because of the terms but because the seller is not committed to relinquishing his most prized possession.

Sometimes the decision process hits a snag. Something holds you back. It could be anxiety about employees, the family name disappearing from the business or loss of independence. A seller doesn't have to relinquish an entire company, especially if keeping a piece eliminates problems or hesitations. A company is composed of pieces and each can be sold or kept. You determine what parts of your operations constitute the sale package. Hold on to personal property, land or buildings, separate divisions or assets if you feel better not selling them. Keeping a piece of your company, as Boyd Hill kept the pneumatic nail distributorship, can make your decision easier and clearer.

You have probably daydreamed dozens of times about selling. It's a common fantasy, right up there with winning the lottery. Over time, the thought returns more and more and you wonder about what you would do without your company. This vision constitutes the threshold and you've crossed it. When you start thinking about what you'll do afterward you've decided to sell.

## UNDERSTANDING HOW BUYERS THINK

> "I almost sold, then backed off at the last minute because of the philosophy of the buyer. I was afraid he would turn it into a voice, a partisan voice pushing right-wing ideology, which I thought would kill the paper. Even though it was a good deal. I guess I was a lot more idealistic. I just dropped the whole thing."　　　—Sidney Yudain

When they think about cashing in, most sellers attach the caveat, "at the right price." There is another condition: "to the right buyer." Before launching a sale, sellers should understand how buyers think, what they want and why. A commitment to sell is meaningless if a seller has an unrealistic or distorted idea of buyers' intentions and goals.

Buyers are complicated animals. They're motivated by things such as quarterly earnings, future profits, tax laws, desire for expansion, fear of competitors, ego, a sense of adventure and a love of deal making. Some are skilled professionals—acquisitions experts who comb the country for targets that meet their formulas and match their master plans. Some acquire companies more often than most people purchase a car. Other buyers purchase a company because of a special situation or liquidation. Each of these sales is unique. It could be as natural as a company taking over its major competitor or as unusual as a publisher yearning to expand into professional baseball.

Some buyers are pure investors. They hunt for companies that generate cash, earnings or tax losses, or are undervalued, or meet other investment goals. These are bottom-line people who don't want to run a company and don't care about its business as long as the numbers are right. Such buyers may want to reshape a company and sell off assets, or expand one segment of its business.

Every buyer is unique, of course, but here are some common reasons behind an acquisition:

- Increase stock value or equity of the acquiring company.
- Secure new sources of supplies or raw materials.
- Diversify into a new line of business or products.
- Move into a new geographical area.
- Benefit from economies of scale in production, distribution and marketing.
- Reduce competition.
- Increase market share.
- Create an impression of expansion.
- Reduce tax liabilities.
- Acquire talented management.
- Acquire unique manufacturing processes or patents.
- Invest earnings from an existing business or to generate income.
- Own one's own business.

Although it's hard to categorize motives neatly, buyers can be split into two major groups: public and private.

Generally, public buyers are responsible to shareholders and Wall Street analysts, meaning they make decisions more slowly than private buyers. The public company may offer stock or corporate notes. And public companies commonly reorganize a new acquisition to fit their operations.

Private investors or corporations usually offer cash or notes (they have no marketable corporate stock to offer) and make quick decisions. Companies with a strong cash flow, few liabilities and no large requirements for capital catch their eye. Many buyers prefer management to remain. Private buyers, because they don't have to publish numbers, can offer higher bonuses and more perks.

Buyers have definite shopping lists, and many use formulas in deciding whether to buy. These formulas are like an overlay on a stencil: if a company matches it the buyer is interested.

A common formula is the *present value method*, or *discounted future cash flow*. This estimates the value of a company by projecting how much cash it will generate in future years and adjusting those figures to the present-day value at a given rate of return. Another method is a *price/earnings* multiple comparing the selling company's stock price and earnings ratio with similar companies that have been sold. Some buyers apply the *net asset value* method, which calculates the value of a company's assets minus liabilities. A fourth formula is *return on assets*. This establishes a minimum acceptable profit before taxes, such as 25 percent, for any potential acquisition.

There are other formulas—accountants delight in coining strings of nouns that bewilder saner minds. Our point is not to suggest memorizing them but to show that buyers use many yardsticks and a savvy seller learns which formula a buyer is applying. Sometimes a public buyer's annual report or 10-K report reveals an acquisition formula. Or you may infer a formula by noting which part of your financials a buyer studies and the direction of questions.

Formulas aside, all buyers ponder the financial structure of a sale. Buyers normally possess three kinds of currency: cash, stock and notes. In scrutinizing an acquisition, they weigh these currencies in order to make the deal that best fits their objectives. Financially strong public companies are often willing to issue whatever type of currency a seller wants.

With these currencies, buyers consider four methods of purchase. Given the changes of the 1986 Tax Reform Act, the first option is the most popular and number 4, the least. Here's how buyers think. Bear in mind, these are not necessarily a seller's standards, but they'll give you an idea of the pros and cons in a buyer's mind.

### 1. *Buyer purchases stock and pays cash.*

PRO
- Paying cash is usually the simplest transaction.
- Licenses, distribution agreements, regulatory approvals, leases and other legal documents don't have to be reassigned to the new owner.
- Only a few of the selling company shareholders may have to agree to the sale, depending on company bylaws, state corporation laws and fairness laws for minority stockholders.
- Buyer may have excess cash or access to cheap financing.
- Cash may have a magic effect on a seller in pricing.

CON
- Buyer's taxes on future earnings may be increased.
- Buyer may be cash-poor.
- Buyer may acquire unknown or undisclosed liabilities.
- Some major stockholders may not want to sell, because they don't want the cash and tax problems.
- Transaction may have to meet disclosure rules of the Securities and Exchange Commission.

### 2. *Buyer exchanges stock for stock.*

PRO
- Seller shares in stock gains or losses.

- Sellers eager to accept stock and defer taxes may accept lower price.
- Buyer holds on to cash and stays liquid.
- Buyer may make many acquisitions and dilute seller's shares.

CON

- Seller may receive a significant portion of the buyer's stock.
- Value of stock, if publicly traded, may increase or decrease, and a buyer has to consider this risk. Buyer's earnings per share have been diluted.
- Transaction has to meet SEC rules for filing and full disclosure.
- Buyer values two companies—the acquirer and the acquisition—instead of one.
- Higher legal and accounting expenses.

### 3. *Buyer purchases assets and pays cash.*

PRO

- Buyer may increase ("step up") tax basis of assets and reduce goodwill on the books. (Buyers don't like goodwill —it can't be amortized and written off. As a result, the buyer has fewer deductions and pays higher taxes.)
- Buyer chooses not to assume responsibility for certain liabilities.
- Buyer generally avoids assuming obligations such as past income taxes, pension plans and severance agreements.
- Buyer avoids undisclosed liabilities.

CON

- Asset purchases may involve complicated valuation, especially if a company has significant intangibles or buyer intends to liquidate part of it.
- Certain liabilities or loan covenants may prohibit a seller from liquidating or selling the assets.
- In a distress sale, buyer has to ensure that titles are clear, liens have been unearthed, and state bulk sales laws have been met.

**4.** *Buyer purchases assets and pays with stock.*

PRO
- Buyer generally avoids assuming unspecified liabilities.
- No cash outlay is required and buyer stays liquid.
- Buyer's stock may be perceived as being worth more than its true value.

CON
- Seller may receive a major interest in the buyer's company.
- Asset purchases may be complicated.
- Loan covenants or liabilities may impede the sale.

## TAXES AND TIMETABLES

A buyer worries about taxes the way a dieter worries about calories: some foods cause him to put on weight and others don't. Some acquisitions add to a buyer's taxes and others do not. Buyers concentrate on their tax basis. Taxes are increased or not affected, depending on how purchased assets are valued for tax purposes.

A buyer frequently seeks tax results that are precisely the opposite of a seller's. While buyers study tax bases, sellers worry about double taxation. When a buyer wants to pay with stock, the seller may prefer to receive cash and to pay taxes rather than defer them and risk higher rates later. Or a buyer may want a taxable asset transaction in order to write off deductions that come with the assets, while a seller may prefer a nontaxable stock transaction. Either way seller and buyer may differ in their tax goals and should be ready to negotiate.

A sale normally takes longer than anyone expects. It can be broken into three stages: Infatuation (Signing of the Letter of Intent), Romance (Performing Due Diligence), and Marriage (Signing the Purchase Agreement). Even with a willing buyer and seller, the courtship can drag on for months.

Let's say two companies look like a natural fit, agree on a ballpark price, and everyone thinks how great it's going to be working together. That's Infatuation, which moves quickly with the signing of the Letter of Intent. The slow part is Romance (Due Diligence). Paper searches and accountants or lawyers invariably dig up new questions to be resolved. The greater the number of lawyers, investment bankers and accountants, the slower the pace. Not only is there wrangling between the buyer's and seller's representatives, but also within each camp. Turf fights and personality conflicts are not unusual. The Marriage Ceremony is either a formal signing with a quick finale, or a grueling multihour marathon in which the two sides piece together a Purchase Agreement.

Expect holdups in a sale and keep current on what is causing them. A buyer who is stalling may not have the money to close the sale. Slow response can be a sign that the buyer lacks financing. A first-time buyer may be having second thoughts about the purchase. Delays tie up your company and keep it off the market. Watch for trouble signs or a buyer who postpones settlement without good cause. There is no average time for a sale. Sixty days is common, and less than a month or more than a year is atypical. The pace is often determined by types of companies—some simply have more complicated businesses, such as international firms or companies covered by environmental regulations.

## ONE SELLER'S STORY: Temporary Services, Inc.

The sale of Temporary Services, Inc., should have transpired quickly. Owner Dee Weitzel prepared her company, found a buyer and began negotiations with the deliberation of a chess player. She expected the process to take six months. Instead, it stretched for more than a year as she and the buyer haggled over taxes. But Weitzel controlled her impatience and got what she wanted.

Located in Grand Junction, the energy capital of western Colorado, TSI grew rapidly in the late 1970s by providing clerical, domestic, and manual labor and professional help to companies arriving for the energy boom. Six years after Weitzel started with $5,000 seed money, TSI was grossing $1.8 million annually, employing fourteen full-time people and managing 1,400 part-time employees. But the energy boom would not last.

Every October she projected the coming year's accounts. In

1981 her usually accurate, conservative estimates fell short. Fewer new clients were moving in and Weitzel foresaw a steep slump. When one of her biggest clients, Exxon U.S.A., closed its oil shale facility and laid off 2,000 workers, she knew it was time to get out. Hard times were coming, and she didn't have the money to survive. Nor could she borrow; she was extended to the limit of her $100,000 bank credit line.

To find a buyer, Weitzel talked to larger temporary agencies in Denver and Salt Lake. She contacted trade associations and obtained industry statistics to value her business. "It's hard to know what a service company is worth," she relates. "All I had was a list of accounts and a marketing strategy. The big ticket was the client list. The statistics showed that service companies were valued on billable hours. Then you factor in things like location and number of years in business."

Weitzel found a Salt Lake City agency, SOS Temporary Services, that wanted to expand into western Colorado. One reason the TSI sale succeeded was that Weitzel thoroughly checked out this buyer. Her questions and research convinced her that SOS could afford the purchase and had sufficient capital to weather the approaching depression. She visited the buyer's offices, asked employees about salaries and received assurances from his banker that he had sufficient cash. "I found out enough so I knew he wasn't just taking me to the dance," she says about their dealings. This buyer could go all the way.

They signed a letter of intent soon after the first meeting. Weitzel next strengthened her bargaining position by grooming her company, giving special attention to her most valuable asset. She remembers, "I made sure that all clients were happy. We really double-timed our client touching so that they were good, solid accounts. I knew that enhancing the client list was important. And during negotiations we landed a great big company—U.S. Steel. Bringing that client on-line while we were in negotiations increased our value."

For all its promise, the sale of TSI floundered for more than a year. Months ticked by as Weitzel and the buyer negotiated over the phone, through the mail and by teleconference with accountants. The obstacle was not the price—the buyer was purchasing

TSI stock for around $200,000. The structure of the price and taxes were the proverbial wrench. The buyer wanted to pay all cash. Weitzel didn't want cash. As a former accountant who had kept the books for a Big Eight accounting firm, she knew tax law. Cash meant a hefty capital gains bill from the IRS.

Weitzel recalls, "The pricing structure wasn't fun. By this time, we had agreed in principle what they were going to pay. But we were hassling right up to the end. They wanted a lot of write-offs at the front end because they were having a really good year with their business. So they wanted to pay as much money at the front end as possible. I had other income from a mining partnership so I didn't want money up front. We ended with a compromise.

"I finally said, 'Tell you what, why don't we get a conference call going here, and we'll let the legal beagles talk to each other and let the accountants talk to each other. They'll figure out what's best for both of us.' And that's what we did." The final arrangement was an elaborate installment sale that gave Weitzel one-fourth of the price in cash. The rest was spread over a one-year employment contract, a one-year payment based on gross earnings and a three-year consulting agreement. Her proprietary instincts still twitching, Weitzel asked for first rights to buy the business back. "That was so they wouldn't turn around and sell it to some national firm and make more money. I wanted them to work it."

Once you know you want to sell and have set reachable goals, your next move is to decide how. How do you make your business saleable? One of Weitzel's smartest moves was sprucing up her company for the bargaining table. By reinforcing her most valuable assets—client relations and healthy receivables—she increased her company's value.

# 2 DRESSING UP

Every company should spruce up for sale. Young or old, small or large, light touches or a thorough workover—dressing up any business enhances its value. Sure it's possible to sell without preparation and many sellers do. But you attract a better price and, not incidentally, construct a better-functioning company when you sharpen its image and operations.

## ONE SELLER'S STORY: Rosecraft, Inc.

When Stephen Rosendorf decided to sell the family business he knew he had to improve the company's retained earnings: "For three to four years I planned on building the company so I could sell it. I saw if I did the right things, played the right games and was not a pig in the business, I could position myself in the marketplace to put together a beautiful company package."

For forty-five years, this East Coast costume jewelry maker and wholesaler fed and clothed two generations of Rosendorfs. Tiny, energetic Natalie Rosendorf, mother and merchant, started assembling trinkets behind a bedroom door in a cramped New York apartment in 1940. She recalls, "That's when I.D. bracelets were hot. We'd go to Providence [the country's costume jewelry capital] in the morning, then set up a counter at Filene's. If you didn't do 'X' amount of business you had to give it up. So you had to have merchandise that sold."

Over the next twenty years Rosecraft Company peddled earrings, bracelets, necklaces and souvenirs at Christmastime. During the other nine months business languished. It reached its first sales milestone—$100,000—in 1960, around the time oldest son Martin started selling accounts as a summer job, and then full-time after he graduated from college.

Like his mother, Martin was a gifted salesperson. Steve sums up his brother's success: "There are four thousand other people selling the same goods you're selling. You're constantly fighting competition. You have to sell yourself, number one, and your product, number two." With Martin leading, Rosecraft sales surged to $2 million.

Then in 1976, Rosecraft suffered a devastating blow: Martin died and twenty-six-year-old Steve had to take command. Steve remembers, "When he died we had maybe twenty people working for us. And suddenly I was responsible and I wasn't about to let anybody down. I put slave labor into the company—obsession and hours. Not that I hadn't before, but I was doing it on a different level. I lived and breathed it. This was food on the table for my wife, my two children, my mother, my father, my brother's wife and his two children."

In his battle to keep the company afloat and overcome the sorrow of Martin's death, Steve made a promise. "My brother was thirty-three and I was twenty-six. One day he was perfectly healthy and six months later he was dead. We thought we were invincible. And I said if it could happen to him it could happen to me. I couldn't see myself working my entire life like he did and then one day die. So I set a goal: live for today, enjoy today, and by the time I'm forty, retire." It was an ambitious target, all the more so because Steve intended to depart with at least $10 million.

Steve drove himself, and the company and sales climbed. Natalie stepped aside, and Steve's father, constantly at odds with his relentless son, also bowed out of the business. "My father and I did not see eye to eye on running the business," Steve explains.

"My father was from the old school: he wanted to make a dollar before he spent a dollar. I would spend two dollars before I made anything, knowing I would make five dollars later."

Methodically, Steve laid the foundation for the sale of Rosecraft and added valuable "extras." He instinctively knew his company had to look good from all angles. To impress customers, he decorated the offices with stylish Art Deco furnishings. He hired four new vice presidents. "I picked people who were better for the job than I was. They had professional backgrounds, were smarter than I was. These were people who could run the company without me."

Next he turned to his financials. Eager to accumulate a bottom-line profit, he pruned expenses. "I wanted more retained earnings. The company was built for our family's personal living. We had no retained earnings, but it didn't make any difference. Then I saw that if I wanted to sell the company Rosecraft had to have an earnings history. So I cut back on expenses while sales continued growing. The company was growing, but I was taking out less and less. I used to spend the profits on good living, until I said I want to sell the company. Six years ago I took everything the company made. Not now."

Steve envisioned leaving Rosecraft with $10 million by taking the company public, and he calculated that the jewelry firm needed to gross $20 million a year before it would be ready. A twist of fate set the sale in motion ahead of his schedule. While he considers the experience a fluke, a surprising number of other company owners say that coincidence or luck played a pivotal role in their sales.

In 1985, as sales were pushing through $13 million, Steve and his wife booked a vacation to Italy, using their frequent-flier credits for first-class tickets. They boarded in New York, and somewhere over the Atlantic Steve struck up a conversation with the business traveler beside him. He happened to be the chairman of one of the country's largest brokerage houses, Prudential-Bache. For the next four hours they talked about Rosecraft. The week Steve returned from Europe he received a call from Pru-Bache with a proposal to underwrite the public offering of Rosecraft, Inc.

From May to November Steve and the brokers assembled the

papers for Rosecraft's public debut. When they got around to valuing the company, Steve deferred to the investment bankers. A common pitfall among sellers is their unfamiliarity with how a business can be valued. Rosecraft was earning $3 million on $13.5 million revenues, and any number of formulas could be used.

Steve says, "I didn't know what price to expect. I had never been involved in a deal like this, so I listened to the brokerage people, outside accountants, my own accountants. They came up with numbers that sounded great to me. The brokers told me the company was worth approximately $36 million. It's a P/E company—you do a multiple of earnings. It was eleven to twelve times earnings."

The public offering promised rich rewards, but timing was everything. Over the months, as the brokers scrambled to ready the company, the offering window shrunk to where the company would garner only eight times earnings. Steve backed away. But mentally and emotionally he was ready to sell.

So he and another arm of Pru-Bache constructed a leveraged buyout. In exchange for selling 49 percent of Rosecraft, he would pocket $10 million cash (to be borrowed with principal and interest paid from Rosecraft earnings) and a note for $8 million (principal and interest also paid by Rosecraft earnings). Steve was both attracted and repelled by the LBO. "It was a very exciting idea because you could do it over and over again. But it was very risky. That's what bothered me the most. I was very nervous with the debt. I felt that a bad quarter or bad six months could put the company out of business."

One week before he signed the papers he was invited to lunch by the president of another jewelry company, Lori Corporation. Industry gossips were whispering that Rosecraft was "doing something financial," the president related, and if Rosecraft was for sale, his parent company, ARTRA Group Inc., would be a willing buyer. "I was very cocky," Steve remembers, "which is unusual for me. I'm usually not. But being ready to sign the LBO, I was in a great position. I explained the deal I had on the table, and that if he wanted the company he had to act quickly."

They lunched on Thursday, and the following Monday Steve

and his wife met with the president to show him through their warehouses and sales operations. To negotiate the price Steve brought in his accountant, and the group gathered in a conference room. Feeling courted and in a no-lose position, Steve was relaxed. "They gave us a price. Then my accountant and I went into the back room, looked at each other and said, 'This is a great offer. Let's see what more we can get.' As soon as the offer was made we loved it, but we didn't want to show it." Smoothing negotiations was the good chemistry between Steve and the buyer. He liked the buyer's values: "It was important to me because I like to know who I'm getting married to. He said he wasn't buying a company, he was buying people." Four hours later Rosecraft had a buyer.

The buyer offered $16 million for Rosecraft, Inc. Although less than the LBO price, it was debt-free. The deal that emerged was $10 million cash, $4 million in two-year notes, $2 million of the buyer's public stock, and an employment contract for Steve that gave him 20 percent of Rosecraft's pretax, predebt earnings over the next five years. They shook hands, and within thirty days the buyer deposited $1 million in Steve's bank account. The remainder of the cash was due in sixty days.

Until this point the sale of Rosecraft was virtually flawless. Only Steve's faith in the buyer and his determination to consummate the deal pushed it to the end. After the buyer made the initial deposit, Steve granted him an extension on the next deadline after learning that the buyer didn't have the cash. "The buyer never came to me personally, but I sensed he was having difficulty. I didn't have to get involved, but I did because it was beneficial for everybody." With Steve's introduction to his banker and Rosecraft as collateral for financing, the sale was completed.

Steve is not yet forty, but that landmark no longer looms. Having defeated the demons of his brother's death, he relishes his new position at Rosecraft. "I could be talked out of retiring at forty," he smiles.

## POLISHING YOUR IMAGE

"Company image" sounds like a vague notion, but it's real and it's critical. Every facet of your company conveys its image. Little things are often most telling: embossed business cards, a secretary reading a novel during working hours, how employees address you, the make of office equipment, even whether you eat at your desk or swim at lunchtime. These all say something about your company's efficiency and profitability.

The sixty-eight-year-old owner of a regional restaurant embellished her company image through casual remarks about her favorite sport. At the first meeting with a buyer, the owner talked about managing individual eateries spread over a four-state region. During a lull in the conversation as a waiter refilled their coffee, the owner recounted a grueling three-set tennis match she had played that morning.

Tennis came up again at the meeting, and at one point the seller invited the buyer to a game of fast singles. The owner wasn't looking for competition—she was image-building. She explains, "I hoped to stay on, so I wanted Dennis to know I was healthy. He could see I wasn't a kid. I didn't want him to wonder whether I was being forced into retiring because of health."

Imagine a buyer visiting your office. What would be the reaction to your office, plant, shop or warehouse? Your surroundings mirror your company's inner workings. Junk, stacks of messy papers, broken furniture, peeling paint—a company mired in disorder looks like it's barely holding its head above water. Forget the reality—that you're growing so fast you haven't time to clear boxes from the hallways—what's important is the appearance.

Here's how you can improve your company surroundings:

- Paint, organize, and remove junk or stacks of papers.
- Replace worn or broken fixtures.
- Showcase products and sophisticated office equipment.
- Clean carpets, walls, machinery and washrooms.
- Straighten and organize inventory.
- Clear hallways or makeshift storage areas.
- Tidy the grounds around the office or employee parking lot.

**Organize company records.**

Time to stop stuffing invoices into the bottom drawer or postponing writing salary guidelines. Collect and compile minutes of board meetings. Generally, the company lawyer arranges the minutes of the first meeting, so missing minutes can be constructed using that format. Check that patents and copyrights are up-to-date and filed with the right government office.

**Even the smallest company needs a policies and procedures manual for employees.**

This manual may be a thick binder or a series of memos—size is unimportant compared with relevance to company operations and employees. Sections should cover general information, personnel, hours and vacations, health insurance, retirement plans and recordkeeping procedures.

## COMPANY LITERATURE

"Our sales document was a pretty thorough explanation of the company. Its history, financials, marketplace, share of the market, competitors, where it had been, where it was going, where it planned to go."
—Bill Lennartz

A brochure makes a company appear prosperous and established. Even the most modest outfit looks impressive when it's illustrated in color and bold type on glossy paper. This handout shows photographs of employees or offices; describes activities, products, marketing, customers and managers; and gives the names of accountants and banking references.

Brochures explain a complex enterprise or demystify esoteric processes or products—experimental research, manufacture of highly technical components, or a specialized service. Buyers want a concrete grasp of a company. If its name is a string of high-tech adjectives and a Dun & Bradstreet synopsis is too general, a clearly written brochure illuminates even the most arcane business.

A brochure would have helped show a multinational sugar grower exactly what he was purchasing and helped him avoid a costly, failed acquisition. This buyer watched his Los Angeles trading company go bankrupt in three years because he didn't understand buying and selling commodities. The buyer identified with farming and warehouses and shipping—not nimble traders juggling prices and jumping in and out of markets. Soon after the acquisition the new owner promised lavish bonuses if traders reached a certain level of sales.

It was like challenging a gambler to beat the blackjack table —with someone else's money. Traders rushed into heavy transactions and extended margins to their limits. When they were caught short the company covered their losses. Eventually, losses buried the company because the buyer didn't know how to gauge levels of risk. The seller also lost because part of the purchase price was contingent on the firm's future profits. The buyer might have saved its $5.3 million investment if it had understood the intricacies of trading and risk and the importance of monitoring traders. A company brochure could have said all this.

Your company brochure can be accompanied by another document. Called a **selling memorandum** or **selling document**, it's a sketch of your company that blends facts and prospects. It summarizes activities and areas of growth, marketing plans and general financial results, and sets forth reasons for selling. Depending on the size of the company, this document can be a single page or an extensive notebook. Some buyers are impressed by lengthy, expensively produced presentations and others prefer a lean synopsis. If you want to keep your sale quiet and confidential, do not put your name on this sheet. Some sellers release a comprehensive package of information to investment bankers or business brokers and let them prepare a memorandum or selling letter for would-be buyers.

The following selling memorandum is an example of a letter sent to prospective buyers. While relatively brief, it gives a buyer enough information to decide whether to pursue the acquisition.

[SAMPLE SELLING MEMORANDUM]

### INVESTMENT DECISIONS
The Magazine for the Financial Professional

*Investment Decisions* is a financial magazine edited for senior business and financial executives. Regular features include articles on corporate finance, money management, portfolio strategy, pension management, investor relations, international finance, corporate services, management strategies and institutional investing.

*BACKGROUND*
*Investment Decisions* magazine was started in the fall of 1981 as a data-based bimonthly journal. The original name of the publication was *Survey of Wall Street Research*. The editorial product was tightly focused on industry research coverage of sixty industry groups.

The publishing proposition was that controlled circulation delivery to security analysts and portfolio managers of editorial material comprising industry-oriented research and industry outlook articles would provide an effective environment for corporate advertisers seeking to build or enhance their image with professional investors.

In the fall of 1983 the circulation was expanded to include senior corporate financial management, and the editorial format was diversified to cover corporate finance, mergers and acquisitions, investment management strategies, pension fund management and real estate.

*CIRCULATION*
The magazine circulation is carefully targeted for virtually every professional in the following categories:

• Corporations—chairmen, presidents, chief financial officers, treasurers, controllers and corporate secretaries at 5,000 companies with annual sales exceeding $40 million.

• Corporation pension, public and other tax-exempt funds—pension officers, advisors, managers, directors, consultants and administrators at all public and private funds with assets over $10 million.

• Financial institutions—chief investment officers, portfolio managers, investment bankers, securities analysts, traders, investment advisors, counselors and consultants at the 1,300 largest banks, the 500 largest insurance companies, 1,200 largest independent investment managers and 600 largest securities firms, including corporate finance executives, department heads, institutional brokers, plus all the directors of research and securities analysts covering sixty industry groups, plus top executives at thrift institutions and important federal and state government officials.

The magazine is audited by the Business Publications Audit of Circulation, and subscriber base is 42,000.

Circulation has grown rapidly, doubling in the two-and-a-half-year period ending December 1985 to 38,000. Reader interest continues high, with circulation up 10 percent to 42,000 as of June 1986.

*Investment Decisions* competes in the advertising marketplace with *Institutional Investor* (estimated U.S. ad revenues, $22 million; circulation, 63,000) and *Pensions and Investment Age* (estimated U.S. ad revenues, $7 million; circulation, 43,000).

The magazine relies on advertising for revenues and has a very modest paid-circulation base. It has not undertaken a paid-subscriptions promotion.

*Investment Decisions* is published eight times a year. The magazine was bimonthly until January 1986, and plans are to increase frequency to monthly, starting with the February issue.

*EDITORIAL*

Each issue of *Investment Decisions* contains three types of editorial material: feature stories by writers with experience and ability in the business and financial fields; monthly departments, produced in-house, covering specific subjects; and a special feature. Special editorial features/directories scheduled are:

*February:* Employee benefits, 401(K) programs, chief financial officers and treasurers.

*April:* Real estate, cash management.

*May:* Investment research, computer products, financial services, annual report section.

*June:* Leasing, asset-based lending, master trustees.

*August:* Corporate finance, investment banking.

*October:* Investment management.

*November:* Large pension and public funds, real estate.

*December:* Pension fund consultants, international investment managers.

*FORMAT*

*Investment Decisions* is produced by four-color web-offset printing and saddle stitch binding. Trim size is 8⅛ by 10⅞ inches.

## A PROFITABLE STRUCTURE

The other half of sprucing up encompasses the structure of a company—management, personnel and financial records.

An attractive structure for a company is the **S Corporation**, especially since enactment of the 1986 Tax Reform Act. In an S Corporation, unlike its better-known sibling the C Corporation, profits and losses pass through to individual shareholders, who pay taxes on them at their personal rates. In a **C Corporation** profits, losses and taxes are paid at the corporate level. This creates a double tax for C Corporation shareholders—their company is taxed on its profits, and they are taxed on their dividends and distributions.

Tax experts generally recommend an S Corp or partnership for a new, privately held company that may someday be sold. They even go so far as to recommend converting an existing company to S Corp status if it may eventually be sold. Noncorporations would not benefit from changing to an S Corp because incomes and expenses already flow to the individual taxpayer. And, with tax rates changed, corporate rates are no longer lower than individual rates. It used to make sense to be a corporation. Today it's not necessarily so—individual rates may be lower.

Another attraction of an S Corporation becomes apparent at selling time. An owner of an S Corporation pays personal income taxes, but the company owes no taxes on gains. (*Note:* this applies only to a sale of company assets. If stockholders of a C Corporation sell their stock, then receipts go directly to shareholders with no stop-off at the corporate level.) In an asset sale, the C Corporation, however, pays taxes on the corporate level, and the shareholder pays personal taxes on the excess over the value of the assets.

Let's say a corporation sells assets with a tax basis of $1 million for $5 million. Shareholders in a C Corporation would see their company taxed on the $4 million gain, and when the remainder was distributed to them they would also owe taxes. Shareholders in an S Corporation would witness only a single tax on them personally. The corporation would not be taxed on the $4 million gain.

S Corporations have limitations—they can issue only one class of voting stock, and no more then thirty-five individuals can be shareholders. Other corporations or Employee Stock Ownership Programs (ESOPs) cannot be shareholders, thus eliminating potential sources of capital. S Corporations are restricted as to the kinds of income they can receive, such as "passive" income. Also, a company must be an S Corporation from its beginning or for three years (ten years starting in 1989) before it can sell as an S Corp, so sellers must plan ahead. Nevertheless, an S Corp structure can pay off.

There is a one-time exception to the tax law and our recommendation for avoiding double taxation. A closely held C Corporation is partially or completely exempted from double taxation if it sells its assets for less than $10 million before 1989. Before January 1, 1989, and assuming the wizards of Capitol Hill don't tinker with current tax law, you can sell your C Corporation for $10 million or less and limit or completely avoid paying both corporate and personal taxes on any gains. After 1988 only an S Corp can avoid double taxation.

*Note:* Qualifying for the "small company exemption" is complex. Some companies selling assets may owe taxes arising from depreciation and investment credit recapture. Sellers should check with their tax advisors.

## REWRITE THE ORGANIZATIONAL CHART

One person often dominates a successful company. Many founders and owners are renowned for keeping a strong grip on daily operations and providing vision and drive. But a company shouldn't be dependent on one person. Buyers want continuity and executives who can manage without the owner.

Buyers know that most sellers leave a company within a few years of their sale. According to acquisition experts, 80 percent of company owners leave their firms within five years of a sale. Founders, start-up artists and entrepreneurs prefer to be their own bosses. Elaborate perks, titles and high salaries can hold on to only a few owners after a couple of years.

Given that most sellers will eventually leave, a buyer does not want a company that will collapse without its founder and leader. A company has to show management depth and that it can generate profits without its master architect.

The organizational chart—titles and lines of accountability—can vividly portray shared authority. Titles spell out control and impose a hierarchy of responsibility. On a company chart, a business owner and four coworkers emerge as president, senior vice president, marketing director, production manager and administrative supervisor.

Assigning titles is not simply window dressing. A farsighted chief executive should groom the second- and third-in-command to run the company after he is gone. By sharing sale plans, a seller can explain benefits and gains and enlist their cooperation. If senior officers do not own substantial equity, a "sale bonus" is a short-term incentive. Negotiating or sharing a bonus pool based on future profitability is another way to assure promotion of the sale.

The support of senior management raises the question, "Do I tell all employees about selling?" Every industry is rampant with rumors. Once they start, you have to do something. Regardless of what you tell employees, they will gossip. They'll speculate about closed-door meetings with lawyers or accountants, requests to assemble confidential papers, the appearance of unexplained visitors, or private meetings away from the office.

Evaluate the probability of a sale. If high, let employees know. Silence or secretiveness makes people uncomfortable and insecure and hurts morale. Anticipating employee worries will check their worst-case fears. A sensible plan is to inform employees when you sign a letter of intent. Reassure them that buyers rarely sweep through a company and replace the entire staff. Buyers know that companies are successful because of good employees—they want to keep them.

## RECRUIT A DISTINGUISHED BOARD OF DIRECTORS

The reputation, title and background of individual board members reflects, and ideally enhances, company identity. A biotech company in Texas founded by a young veterinarian invited a university professor to the board to add credibility to its research. A San Francisco sporting goods marketer wanted to look international and expand into the Pacific Basin, so he added a Japanese board member. Directors who are bankers, accountants, lawyers and brokerage executives lend an air of professionalism and practicality. In a partnership or proprietorship, a board of advisors impresses the same way.

At selling time the board lineup is fixed, so sellers should examine the composition of their boards beforehand. Recruit directors selectively. Include outsiders. Don't enlist only family members or personal friends with no business expertise. Build a board carefully, person by person, the way you would put together an all-star team. An opportune time to do so is when you branch into new markets or need expert advice and know the kind of person you want. Directors are not pure window dressing. In smaller companies they provide substantive advice and act as good sounding boards.

## ONE SELLER'S STORY: Sun Valley Ski Resort

When William Janss was putting together his board of directors he had specific qualities in mind. The people had to know skiing, be free to attend regular meetings in secluded Ketchum, Idaho, and have a business background. Although he wasn't assembling a star-studded board to impress buyers, the group proved instrumental in the eventual sale.

Sun Valley Ski Resort was like an aging movie star when Janss bought it. It had a glamorous name, but beneath the makeup was a sleepy village, antiquated chair lifts and a run-down inn. "It was an old, tired company with tired people and union-oriented," Janss says about the property of Union Pacific Railroad. But Janss had a dream. Not a dream of making millions or forging a mountain empire, but of creating the world's finest ski resort. Despite the deterioration and money melting at a rate of $750,000 a year, Janss would fashion Sun Valley into a first-class Alpine retreat.

Janss possessed a unique combination of experience: he knew skiing both as a racer and a businessman. As a young man he raced on the Stanford University ski team and the 1940 U.S. Olympic Team. When his days as a downhill racer ended he surveyed ski slopes from another vantage point, as a real estate developer. Active in Aspen's ski boom in the 1950s, he and a partner explored beyond the steep runs of Ajax Mountain and discovered nearby a longer, broader mountain. Locals called the area Brush Creek—Janss called it Snowmass. Parcel by parcel, the Janss Corporation accumulated enough acreage to build Snowmass Village and ski area.

When he acquired Sun Valley, Janss recruited directors with diverse backgrounds—the president of an investment company, a real estate developer, a publishing vice president in charge of marketing and a vice president of a local bank. "They were people of all disciplines and they imposed strong financial control," Janss says.

Janss dedicated ten years to his mountain vision. He erected new ski lifts, renovated the inn, laid eighteen modern tennis courts and converted Sun Valley into a four-season resort earning $500,000 yearly. "We had done it—we built a whole new city, a complete European, state-of-the-art resort. We brought back the World Cup races, we created summer, we built modern tennis courts, an Olympic swimming pool. Everything to make it a major, all-year resort. We had the best of everything."

Having fulfilled his dream, Janss resolved to sell. He hired the investment banking firm of Lehman Brothers (now Shearson Lehman Brothers) to *evaluate* the resort, *value* it and find a buyer. To ascertain the value, the investment bankers examined assets— 2,000 acres, thirty-year leases to property owned by the U.S. Forest Service, equipment and buildings. The investment bankers' primary criterion was not the usual yardstick—a multiple of the resort's annual earnings—but the sale prices of similar resorts. The investment bankers concluded that Sun Valley was worth $15 million to $18 million.

Lehman Brothers produced a steady stream of hotel and resort companies, including Marriott and Disney, to study the Sun Valley books and troop through the inn. Yet it was two years before Janss received his first firm offer, and during this time he grew disenchanted with his investment banker. He felt Lehman Brothers didn't understand the ski resort business. "I expected him to be like Father," Janss remembers about his expectations for an omniscient advisor. Typically, investment bankers get the ball rolling in terms of valuation and introducing sellers to the world of buyers. They provide advice, negotiation skills, and direction, but ultimately an owner makes the final call.

The first serious prospect was Walt Disney Company. Janss was delighted: "They really know how to handle crowds—they're first-class resort operators." Negotiations progressed to closing until the Disney chairman called it off.

Some buyers are window-shoppers, and they can be hard for a seller to spot. Janss recalls, "You're at the mercy of people looking at you, and you have to present them with all the information and presume they are buyers. They [Disney] had the resources to do it and they had talked about having a ski resort. They were here for a full month, watching the operation. They were probably shopping a bit, coming in and seeing how a ski resort worked."

Sometimes buyers themselves don't realize they will never consummate a sale. Janss believes that the Disney staff was eager to buy Sun Valley, but that the chief decision-maker, the chairman, was not. And in any sale a seller has to identify and persuade that one key person. Another tip-off was that Disney Company was not already in the ski resort business. Sun Valley would have been a major diversion.

The first firm offer for Sun Valley came from its board of directors. Two directors proposed buying two-thirds of the company with Janss retaining one-third. "I quoted them a rock-bottom price," he reveals. "They were friends and I thought I would be staying on and working with them." His revised figure was $12.7 million.

Despite the markdown the deal fell apart. One of the directors joined a real estate development in southern California and the prospect of purchasing Sun Valley faded. Janss was in an awkward spot. Having agreed to sell for under $13 million, he felt he could not revert back to the higher price. And discussions about the sale of Sun Valley were reported in the *Wall Street Journal*, so the company was "in play."

Asking a dowry of $12.7 million, the prospective bride didn't have to wait long for another suitor. The next proposal came from an individual investor with extensive holdings in oil, hotels and resorts. Janss knew the man by reputation and checked his business and financial background. He discovered that his new buyer "was a very rich man." Confident that he was dealing with a buyer who was financially qualified and the principal decision-maker, Janss readily agreed to sell.

The buyer offered all cash for most of the resort's assets and properties. (If he had bought Sun Valley stock he would have assumed all assets and liabilities, including, and most importantly, ten separate union contracts. The buyer didn't want to inherit those obligations.) Sale terms contained a significant caveat. In the Idaho courts was a suit challenging Sun Valley ownership. Until this suit was resolved, half the purchase money would be in escrow.

Accrued interest usually eases the sting of an escrow deposit, which locks up a seller's money for months or even years. Though the money may be tied up, at least it's earning something. But in Janss's case interest was not part of the escrow arrangement. And although the suit was eventually dismissed, it tangled the sale for two years and cost Janss millions by undermining the sale terms, not to mention adding legal fees. Janss figures he could have received $3 million more if it were not for the suit.

Negotiations were probably affected by other factors. That winter the snow was thin and resort income depressed. Sun Valley did not look its best. On top of this, Janss was battling a bad head cold that lasted for weeks. "It was debilitating," he remembers, "and it kept me away from negotiations."

Despite frustration over the litigation Janss pushed forward: "I went ahead to try to give him the best package. I wanted Sun Valley to succeed and go on." Lawyers representing both sides assessed the Sun Valley assets and reviewed property lines and titles. Included in the agreement was a six-year consulting contract for Janss, although no duties were specified. Buyers like to assign part of a purchase price to consulting agreements or employment contracts because they can deduct the payments as a business expense (assuming they survive the scrutiny of the IRS).

Because this was an asset sale, Janss could retain ownership to select properties. He wanted to stay in Sun Valley so he kept the title to his house and real property around it. He bargained for access to other assets—lifetime passes for three generations of Janss's to all the resort's recreation facilities. Accompanied by a team of lawyers, Janss closed on the sale within a month of the first meeting with the buyer.

In hindsight, Janss would have done the deal differently. "I would have narrowed the package and taken out land that I wanted to keep. It wouldn't have made any difference in the price. The buyer was not a land man—he was a hotel buyer. I should have had two prices: one for everything (land, buildings) and one just for the resort, just the operations. And I should have settled the suit rather than let it delay the sale."

He wishes he had bargained better. Recalling the buyer's technique, he says, "He would isolate me, asking for concessions. I should have had my lawyers around. I was too accommodating."

## INSURANCE REASSURES BUYERS

In this age of asbestos, the Dalkon Shield and dioxin roads, the specter of devastating personal and environmental liability suits haunts not only sellers but also buyers. These suits are especially frightening because they can appear years after an alleged injury or damage, and everyone, current as well as past owners, can be liable. Heightening fears is the concept of "joint and several" liability, meaning that anyone involved in an action, no matter how small their part, shares liability.

In most instances, insurance for environmental liability is impossible to secure, even though other kinds of coverage may be available. The best protection involves thorough recordkeeping and compliance with all state and federal regulations. A seller can protect a company against suits brought by individuals or employees, or as a result of accidents or product defects. Not only is such coverage good business practice, but it also reassures buyers. For some companies—businesses such as amusement parks, gas stations, or food and drug producers—personal or product liability coverage is basic. A buyer expects to see policies. But some not-so-obvious businesses, such as a public relations firm with extensive libel coverage, are more attractive if they have comprehensive coverage. Insurance makes a buyer feel an acquisition is less risky and protected from costly lawsuits.

## FINANCIALS

"When we started the business we didn't use a lawyer. We sent away for one of those little books. And that's the worst thing in the world to do. Anybody starting a business, the best thing to do is get a lawyer and accountant and get them to help start your business. If you have faith in the business, then you'll spend the money. We started on $300."
— Shannon Edwards

One of the first documents a buyer asks to see is your **financials**. These sum up the real company story—past, present and future. They should be prepared either by an accountant or a certified public accountant, preferably an outsider. If company equity exceeds $1 million, financials should be audited by an independent certified public accountant. Inadequate financials may reduce the purchase price, produce large accounting bills for a special audit, or even kill a sale if they're unbelievable.

If you have just been using a bookkeeper, retain an accountant before talk of a sale. Waiting until the last minute can be costly. A one-time audit may have to reach back three years and will not include an unqualified opinion because past inventory can't be verified. A qualified opinion may reduce your valuation and weaken your demands.

Financial records should chronicle the past three years. Better yet, the past five. The accountant should prepare statements of income and expenses; assets and liabilities and retained earnings; and sources and application of funds (similar to cash flow). If figures are unaudited the accountant's letter provides numerous disclaimers and reasons for them.

If a small company cannot afford an audit, an outside accountant should prepare and present statements on his or her professional stationery. Figures presented by an outside accountant are generally more credible than those of a company employee.

A larger company needs a full-fledged annual audit. Though costly, an audit by a reputable local firm will probably cost less than that of a Big Eight accounting firm. Either way, the expense is justified. Audits are an investment. They gild a company's value by confirming it is healthy and well-managed. An audit is a company's stamp of respectability. It adds dollars to any sale price and reduces the time a buyer spends on due diligence. Buyers are more inclined to accept valuations based on audited statements. With an audit in hand, they're more confident that a seller is presenting a company honestly and accurately.

In recent years many profitable companies have written "zero" in the space for retained earnings. Some owners use their companies primarily to generate a rich lifestyle. Instead of hanging on to profits, owners have opted to minimize their taxes through generous bonuses, benefit plans, profit sharing, liberal entertainment accounts or plush offices. In short, they funneled excess receipts into good living. Although the 1986 Tax Reform Act curtailed some of these payments, some companies still look profitless.

While a company thus saves on taxes by logging more deductions, it keeps none of its profits in the business. Trouble arises when a buyer wants to value a company according to reported earnings and net worth, and the cupboard is bare. An owner may claim that an enterprise has been generating robust profits—which were spent rather than saved. This argument may not be convincing.

The thinking of a New England recruitment firm that parlayed a robust company into conspicuous consumption is typical. Owned and managed by a father and daughter, the business picked up the tab for German cars, weekend meetings at expensive resorts and four-star meals. Annual salaries alone took a $400,000 bite from a $1.3 million gross revenue pie. And usually, on December 31, the company had little left over.

When the owners announced the company's sale, they pointed to part of their salaries as the company's true profits. Potential buyers were skeptical. Maybe the business wouldn't have thrown off such hefty revenues if the top people had been paid less. Perhaps fat salaries were necessary for contacts and contracts, and a new owner would have to pay the same salaries for the same level of income.

To quell such doubts, owners should avoid the Buried Profits Syndrome. Don't run a company hand-to-mouth with enough in the bank to cover only a month's rent and supplies. A company with a growing net worth is the goose that lays tomorrow's golden egg. Retaining profits not only cushions against hard times but is also money in the bank when you sell.

Although a seller can't turn back the clock and recapture spent profits, previous years' statements can be reshaped. If a company is rich in assets and poor in earnings, and a buyer wants earnings power or sizable return on assets, the seller prepares another version of the financials.

A seller can work up **pro forma** statements recasting (sometimes called **normalizing**) its financial history by adjusting individual figures. An accountant rewrites financials by subtracting portions of expenses and adding the difference to the refigured bottom line. On a profit-and-loss statement, line items that may be reduced are salaries, wages and bonuses; intercompany rentals; travel and entertainment; motor vehicle expenses; family directors' and consulting fees; club dues and subscriptions; nonbusiness interest; and ego advertising. The following pro forma is a sample of the kind of statement an accountant prepares to restate company expenses and earnings. This type of statement shows a buyer where cuts can be made and profits improved.

[SAMPLE PRO FORMA]

TEENS AND COMPANY
AND
SUBSIDIARIES
Statement of Income and Expenses
for the Year Ended December 31, 1988

|  | ACTUAL | ADJUSTED |
|---|---|---|
| SALES | $2,870,000 | $2,870,000 |
| COST OF SALES | 1,722,000 | 1,722,000 |
| GROSS PROFIT | 1,148,000 | 1,148,000 |
|  |  |  |
| OPERATING EXPENSES |  |  |
| Salaries and wages | 389,000 | 301,000 |
| Commissions | 201,000 | 182,000 |
| Payroll taxes | 46,000 | 35,900 |
| Employee benefits | 62,000 | 48,360 |
| Rent | 129,000 | 129,000 |
| Insurance | 9,000 | 9,000 |
| Advertising | 12,000 | 10,000 |
| Travel and entertainment | 88,000 | 57,000 |
| Administration | 41,000 | 37,000 |
|  |  |  |
| OTHER EXPENSES |  |  |
| Interest | 26,000 | 26,000 |
| Depreciation | 36,000 | 36,000 |

| | | |
|---|---|---|
| TOTAL EXPENSES | $1,039,000 | $ 871,260 |
| INCOME BEFORE PROVISION FOR TAXES ON INCOME | 109,000 | 276,740 |
| PROVISION FOR TAXES ON INCOME | 29,890 | 107,050 |
| NET INCOME | $ 79,110 | $ 169,690 |

Any expense can be pared if you convincingly argue that company performance would not have suffered. Lease expenses can be cut if the lessor may have charged less, as when the landlord is also the company owner. Interest on loans for nonessential construction may be separated from interest for loans for working capital and then erased from the expense column. To reinforce assertions about profits and returns, a seller can include industry average figures (assuming they are consistent with the revised numbers).

*Caution: Edited financial statements may be hazardous to your company's health.* A rewritten financial history, with a qualification from the accountant, may not be credible. There is another hazard in reborn financials—the Internal Revenue Service. A company that recalculates expenses and beefs up profits for past years may expose itself to additional taxes on the increased earnings. The IRS may contend that high salaries paid to company stockholders were, in reality, dividends and tax them. Or it may apply a company's excess salaries to the company's income and assess additional corporate taxes. At its worst, the IRS can charge interest and penalties or even allege fraud.

The empty space beside **retained earnings** may have to stay that way. In this case, you steer a buyer away from valuations based on past profits and establish a price based on other qualities such as future earning power or market share and growth.

## RAZZLE-DAZZLE

"The [buyer's] corporate treasurer expected to see a five-year plan when he arrived. We informed him that we had been doing well with an idea of what would go on a month from now, let alone five years. Obviously we didn't have one, but we set to work preparing one. Nothing was going to happen until we did."     —Carl von Sternberg

Every company must have a glint of gold to catch a buyer's eye. The glint may be the romantic aura of a company that trades in the Orient, promise of fabulous profits from a technological breakthrough, or total dominance of a market. The glint acts like a Royal Coachman on a hungry trout—with the right lure, a buyer will jump at your company. Often a young company's best bait is its future—coming achievements and earnings. Whether your company is young with a spotty past performance or established with steady growth, it can entice a buyer looking for a richer future.

Illustrate your company's future through a five-year strategic plan. This plan is limited only by your imagination. Highlight company talent in selling a unique product or point out how it's different from competitors. Chart financial growth and attach descriptions of how higher levels of sales, revenues, earnings and assets will be attained. While many buyers discount projections, showing that your company has met or surpassed previous performance targets may give your predictions more credence.

Reinforce financial forecasts with accounts of how your company will expand into new markets, beat out competitors, invent, develop or manufacture new products, revolutionize a service, produce larger volumes, utilize economies of scale, conduct innovative research, acquire new clients and contracts, open new offices, or build new facilities.

Show where expenses will diminish, liabilities will be paid off or shrunk, and profits will pile up. This is the place to put your best projections for your company on paper in convincing detail.

## AN ASSESSMENT CHECKLIST

Knowing what to spruce up means showcasing your company's strengths and its rosy future—and presenting a balanced picture of problems and weaknesses. Are profits on the rise? Is the balance sheet getting stronger? How do costs compare with those of competitors? In short, what are company trends? Smart buyers will form their own answers to these questions.

What follows is an assessment checklist for evaluating your company. You can't spruce up unless you know what's there. Recognizing the bright spots, as well as the black holes, will present your company in the best light.

I. **Structure**
   A. Is your company a partnership, sole proprietorship or corporation?
   B. If a corporation, what kind? What classes of stock has it issued? Who owns stock and how much?
   C. Do state corporation laws impose any restrictions on mergers, liquidation or sale of stock?
   D. Do you have complete records of meetings of the board of directors and stockholders?
   E. What rights do minority shareholders have?
   F. Do corporate bylaws or amendments influence company sale?

II. **Business Activity**
   A. What is your main line of business/products and position in the marketplace?
   B. What is your market share?
   C. What marketing/sales strategies do you use?
   D. What are your market risks?
   E. Who are your competitors and what market share do they control?
   F. Do you own any patents, trademarks, copyrights or other proprietary rights?
   G. What cyclical or seasonal influences affect business?
   H. What factors will influence your prices and terms: taxes,

tariffs, labor costs, production costs, competition, demand, other?

I. When do you need capital the most, and what are the causes of these peaks?

J. Customers and clients: Who are they? Any long-term contracts? How are you increasing them?

K. What is your inventory turnover rate? When do backlogs occur?

L. What is the condition and age of equipment, machinery and facilities? What property or equipment do you lease and what are the terms?

M. What quality control do you apply?

N. What research and development projects are under way? What is their cost, schedule and likely outcome?

## III. Employees/Personnel

A. Who has an employment contract and what are the terms?

B. How long have employees been with the company? What special skills do they have?

C. How do you compensate officers and sales personnel?

D. What bonus plans and/or stock options do you have?

E. Do you use outside consultants or services?

F. What union contracts do you have?

G. Describe insurance, retirement and pension plans.

H. Are there any workers' compensation claims against the company? Any other employee-related suits or claims?

## IV. Finances

A. Who audits the books and financial statements?

B. What method of accounting and inventory control do you use? (LIFO, FIFO, etc.)

C. What internal checks are in place?

D. What internal reports are produced and by whom?

E. Who manages expenses and capital expenditures, and how?

F. What budgeting procedures or estimates do you require?

G. What taxes do you pay and what is your effective rate?

H. What influences your taxes and can they be lowered?

<table>
<tr><td>CHAPTER<br><br>**3**</td><td># ASSEMBLING<br># A TEAM</td></tr>
</table>

"Never go into a sale by yourself. There are just too many areas to be covered. You need reinforcements. I felt strength with my accountant and attorney there."
— Boyd Hill

Merger and acquisition artists are everywhere. Morning papers bulge with double-page spreads heralding the coups of investment bankers. Business owners are bombarded by telephone calls, "personal" letters and promotional flyers from people eager to sign them as clients and sell their company.

These communiqués carry a hard sell. One form letter begins, "Dear Sir, There is going to come a time when you want to sell your business, and at that time you will want honest answers to three questions: What is my business worth? How can I get more for it? Who could manage the sale?" The letter devotes four pages to the services of a company specializing in business sales. Brochures announcing seminars use photographs of multimillion-dollar checks and headlines such as "HOW TO SELL YOUR BUSINESS FOR THE MOST PROFIT."

It's easy to be turned off by the hype and high pressure. No one can miss that these people are selling themselves first and foremost. But behind the billboards are valuable experience and useful advice. At some point in your sale, you'll need help. You cannot avoid using outsiders, so choose carefully.

These people possess all sorts of titles, degrees and expertise. They're investment bankers, business brokers, finders, brokerage firm executives, lawyers, accountants, management consultants, appraisers and acquisition specialists. They find and screen buyers, prepare financials and other documents, value companies, and negotiate and execute agreements with buyers. In short, they do everything for your sale but break the news to your kids.

This raises our main caveat about outside advisors: they are experts in law, finance, accounting, acquisitions and buyers, but usually not your business. A seller should listen to these experts but make the final decision. They provide facts and consequences —point out laws, prepare figures, research what other companies are selling for, check buyers, arrive at a market value for your company, and sit beside you in negotiations. You, however, make the business decisions.

The titles and functions of outsiders often overlap. With few exceptions, they don't undertake a single, discrete task, then bow out of a sale. They may have a specialty such as valuation or financing or appraisals, but they become as deeply involved as you allow. Whether called investment bankers or acquisition lawyers or simply business brokers, they'll do whatever they can to complete a sale at the highest price. They're hired guns, they're fiscal wizards, they're handholders—they're whatever you need.

Most sellers require outside help. Exactly who and how much depends on the seller's expertise, the size of the transaction, who is available and their skills. For smaller transactions and companies away from large cities, business brokers or finders are frequently hired to locate a buyer, and accountants are used to execute a sale. An attorney experienced in acquisitions can help a seller prepare documents and negotiate a sale. Small or regional firms—called **second-tier investment bankers**—advise on all aspects of a sale and put together an offering brochure. Second-tier firms do more than business brokers and less than large investment banking companies or Big Eight accounting firms with acquisition departments.

## BUSINESS BROKERS AND FINDERS:
## BIRD-DOGGING BUYERS

A **finder** locates and introduces buyer and seller; this person may also act as a go-between throughout a sale. **Business brokers** also find buyers and bring companies together, as well as deliver sale proposals, act as the seller's representative and sit through negotiations.

In a sale involving hard assets such as property and buildings, business brokers in some states must have real estate licenses. Without a license, they may not be able to collect their commission. Their commission may also be withheld, depending on state law, if they do not have a written agreement with a buyer or seller. In most states, business brokers are unlicensed. Consequently, their experience, skills and professionalism vary greatly from firm to firm. As with any unregulated service, it's buyer beware or, in this case, seller beware.

An agreement with business brokers and finders can be **exclusive, exclusive agency** or **nonexclusive**. It establishes who represents a seller and receives compensation. Exclusive means that one person represents a seller and receives a commission from a sale to *any* buyer, regardless of who made the introduction. In an exclusive agency agreement, the business broker or finder receives a commission for any sale, unless the seller found the buyer. If the agreement is nonexclusive, a seller pays a commission to anyone acting as an intermediary.

Finders or business brokers are usually paid a 5 to 12 percent commission on sale prices not exceeding a couple of million dollars. The lower the sale price, the higher the percentage. In small transactions with a purchase price under $1 million, business brokers or finders may ask for a minimum fee. In contrast, multimillion-dollar transactions may be handled by investment bankers for 1 percent or less. Fee arrangements include questions about when the money is paid and how the ultimate purchase price is determined.

Fees are complicated when a seller doesn't know the final purchase price, as with an earn-out that bases part of the price on future earnings. Or cash may not be immediately payable or available, as in an installment sale. Stock swaps between seller and buyer can also twist fee arrangements. Fee contingencies should be anticipated in the business broker's or finder's agreement. And regardless of any written or stated policy, all fees are negotiable.

Either side assumes responsibility for a business broker's or finder's fee, depending on who initiated the contact and their agreement. However, many buyers do not like messing with broker's fees and avoid sellers who won't pay them. Occasionally a buyer and seller split the fee. Or a seller can sidestep it. If a seller pays from a company account and doesn't reduce the purchase price by the same amount, the fees have cost nothing.

What follows is a sample exclusive agency broker agreement that illustrates the variable, negotiable points.

---

[SAMPLE BUSINESS BROKER AGREEMENT]

[LETTERHEAD STATIONERY]

The undersigned Owner(s) hereby grant to Brokers & Company, for a period of _____ from the date of this agreement, the sole and exclusive right to sell the following described property:

_____

_____

_____

which the Owners agree to sell at the following price and terms:

_____

_____

_____

or at such other price and upon such other terms as the Owners may accept.

Brokers & Company agrees to use its best efforts and diligence to procure a purchaser for said property, and the Owners agree to cooperate in every possible way, showing the property to all prospective purchasers which Brokers & Company may bring or send, and to refer to it any communications or proposals submitted to the Owners by any prospective purchaser from any source whatsoever during the period of this agreement.

Except for the following persons who have previously contacted the Owners with regard to purchasing said property, any purchaser contacted by Brokers & Company or who contacts or is contacted by the Owners during said period, shall be considered to have been procured by Brokers & Company.

In the event a purchaser is procured for said property within the above period of time, Brokers & Company shall be entitled to a commission, due and payable in full by the Owners at time of closing, as follows:

| Sale Price | Commission |
|---|---|
| Below $250,000 | 8% of price and $7,500 minimum |
| $250,000 to $1 million | 6% of price |
| part of price over $1 million | 5% |
| part of price over $2 million | 4% |
| part of price over $3 million | 3% |
| part of price over $5 million | 2% |
| part of price over $7 million | 1% |

Said commission shall be payable in the event of a sale during said period or within one year thereafter to a purchaser procured by Brokers & Company.

The Owners agree to notify Brokers & Company of the time and place of, and the party conducting the settlement. The Owners shall direct and authorize the party making settlement to deduct the aforesaid brokerage commission from the proceeds of sale and to pay the same directly to Brokers & Company.

In the event legal action is necessary to collect any unpaid brokerage commission, Owners shall pay a service charge of one and one-half percent per month from time of settlement on that commission as well as any additional expenses of collection including reasonable attorney's fees.

In the event that a deposit toward the purchase price is made by a purchaser procured by Brokers & Company who thereafter defaults and the deposit is retained by the Owners or on their behalf, then Brokers & Company shall be entitled to receive from the Owners one-half of the deposit or one-half of the commission to which it would have been entitled if said sale were executed, whichever is less.

The Owners represent that they now are the owners of the property and shall convey it to a purchaser procured by Brokers & Company under the terms of this agreement.

During the period specified above, this agreement shall be irrevocable. If at the end of said period no purchaser has been procured, Brokers & Company shall thereafter have an open and nonexclusive right to obtain a purchaser and shall receive the aforesaid commission on any sale made to the purchaser procured by it. The nonexclusive right to act as a broker may be terminated in writing by the Owners at any time before a purchaser is procured by Brokers & Company.

This agreement shall inure to the benefit and bind the respective heirs, executors, administrators, assigns and successors of the parties hereto.

IN WITNESS WHEREOF, we do hereby set our hands and seals this _____ day of _____, 198_.

Accepted:

Brokers & Company

By _____    _____

(Authorized Agent)

_____

(Owners)

## INVESTMENT BANKERS: THE DEAL MAKERS

Investment bankers are to brokers what turkeys are to chickens —not only bigger and more vocal, but also great for special occasions and good for days and days. While anyone can call him or herself an investment banker, investment bankers usually have legal or accounting backgrounds and experience in corporate finance. They concentrate on the financial aspects of a sale: valuation, preparing financial statements, structuring a price and arranging financing. Money is their specialty, but they also find and screen buyers, conduct an auction or solicit bids to sell a company, and guide negotiations.

Not all sellers need an investment banker. Their cost and expertise may be unnecessary or too overwhelming for a deal. Before deciding *which* investment banker, a seller must decide *whether* he or she needs one.

In many respects, investment bankers are marketers. They wrap a company and its fiscal history in the most attractive package possible, help the seller write the price tag, then find a buyer to pay it. They become deeply involved with a company, scrutinizing operations and finances and preparing the selling memorandum and other documents. Their help may be essential in putting together a comprehensive and enticing selling memorandum. Experienced investment bankers know what these documents must contain and what buyers demand. They tell a seller whether financials should cover three or five years, which executives a buyer would be most interested in keeping, and which products to emphasize.

Investment bankers also play a part in negotiations, sitting beside the seller to bargain each point of the sale. Sometimes they lead negotiations, especially for sellers who are uncomfortable with their own trading skills and prefer the investment banker's cooler, less emotional approach. They're helpful, too, as buffers or go-betweens when negotiations break down or in clearing up misunderstandings.

In a sale involving employee stockholders, outsider stockholders or public stockholders, sellers may want an investment banking firm to render a **fairness opinion** on their decision. This opinion reassures minority stockholders that no financial conflict of interest influenced the seller and they received fair value for the company. (A seller may ask counsel to provide a separate opinion for the buyer on the legality of the sale.)

Investment bankers work for a retainer, commission or contingency fee based on a sale price. A frequently mentioned fee structure is the **Lehman formula.** This is a sliding scale that works thus: 5 percent on the first $1 million of the sale price, 4 percent on the next million, 3 percent on the next million, 2 percent on the next million, and 1 percent on $4 million and up. Fees for sales above $5 million are under 1 percent or less. Applying this formula, a company that sells for $5 million would produce a $150,000 fee ($50,000 + $40,000 + $30,000 + $20,000 + $10,000). A variation on this formula is the addition of a premium, such as $50,000 plus 4 percent on sales of more than $1 million, $90,000 plus 3 percent on sales of more than $2 million, and so on.

Despite its notoriety the Lehman formula is not used that much by the large Wall Street investment bankers. Smaller intermediaries or second-tier firms are more likely to use it.

Often investment bankers quote no fixed fees. Instead they work on an hourly basis (common rate: $150 to $300 an hour) or on retainer (starting anywhere between $35,000 and $100,000). Sellers should bear in mind that fees may not be significantly less for a small transaction, because these can be as complex and time-consuming as a large sale. On top of the hourly fees or retainers, investment bankers may bargain for a **success bonus,** or **performance fee.** This is a percentage of the sale price and is entirely negotiable.

Investment banker's fees are as negotiable as automobile sticker prices. They all depend on the model, whether you want air-conditioning or jeweled mud flaps, loan costs, and how eager the salesman is for the business.

At the end of this chapter is an example of an **engagement letter.** It sets forth terms for fees, expenses, indemnification and services for the sale of a company. Although thick with legalese and dense with one-sentence paragraphs, the letter presents a clear picture of how investment bankers work. Many points are negotiable; sellers shouldn't assume that legal boilerplate makes the agreement ironclad. This is an example—each investment banking firm has its own agreement form it tailors for a sale.

## ONE SELLER'S STORY: Allen Corporation

For years, colorful four-page flyers from a merger and acquisition firm had been landing on the desk of Carl von Sternberg, founder and owner of Allen Corporation in Alexandria, Virginia. Unlike the more conservative pin-stripe houses, this second-tier M & A company had a gimmick: it was peddling a two-day seminar that could add, "hundreds of thousands—even millions—to the price your company will bring in the marketplace." For years, von Sternberg tossed the flyers into the wastebasket.

The calendar finally motivated him to save the flyers. He says, "I would never have sold this company if I was ten years younger, but being fifty-six I knew I had to do something. I'm not going to live forever. There would be nothing worse than to leave my heirs a private company that doesn't have a ready market. I got obsessed with that idea. I had to do something."

Like any business person who has built a multimillion-dollar company from scratch, von Sternberg was skeptical about what an outsider could teach him. Nevertheless, just to pick up a few tips, he enrolled in a two-day seminar conducted by Geneva Corporation, an investment banking and acquisitions firm. "I was quite arrogant," he confesses. "I thought I knew the economics of the business corporation, all the ins and outs. But I was just a babe in the woods. There were so many things I wasn't thinking about, that I hadn't considered." Exposed to the arcane world of forecasting, pro formas and operating ratios, von Sternberg became a convert and hired outside help to sell Allen Corporation.

Allen Corporation designs and analyzes high-technology training programs for the Department of Defense, NASA and aerospace companies. Von Sternberg founded the firm in 1975 with $5,000 and one employee. By the time he was considering selling, annual revenues were growing 50 percent a year and had just rocketed through $12 million. They would hit $18 million the following year.

Earnings were typical for a government contractor that works on a cost plus fixed percentage basis—around 5 percent.

The value of Allen Corporation was an immediate concern to von Sternberg because he had already been approached by one of his clients, Singer Company. Singer had put out feelers before, but this time both parties were primed. Two Singer men, including the vice president for business development, visited von Sternberg's office late one afternoon. They immediately raised the subject of Allen joining Singer. Von Sternberg listened to their vision of the new entity, then voiced his doubts. Could his company, which analyzed training programs, maintain independence if it were owned by Singer, a manufacturer of those very programs?

Von Sternberg was eager to know how much his company might garner. But he kept quiet, sensing that a seller should not seem ignorant about the value of his company. He should appear confident of its worth, regardless of his uncertainties. The men left, promising to be back.

Von Sternberg hired Geneva to examine his books while two New York brokerage houses examined Allen Corporation's value. The brokers were considering taking the company public. Von Sternberg paid nothing for the brokerage firms' valuations. But if he went through with a public offering, the lead firm would receive a fee through the underwriting and sale of the stock. As the three teams marched along on parallel courses, von Sternberg negotiated with Singer.

"Since they came to us, the ball was pretty much in their court," von Sternberg says. Forcing a buyer to take the initiative by acting only mildly interested can be an effective strategy. "They did their best in subsequent meetings to convince me that they would allow us to continue to be objective and independent and not be influenced by the hardware components of their company. Obviously, they convinced me."

Von Sternberg met regularly in New York and Virginia with the Singer vice president. The first mention of money came in the bar of a hotel on Central Park in the middle of a weekday afternoon. "We just talked about the total amount," von Sternberg remembers. "No point in talking details unless the amount was proper. I said I'd consider it."

Unknown to Singer, von Sternberg already had a number in hand. The investment firm Smith Barney Harris Upham and Company had declared Allen Corporation stock to be worth $10 million.

Pricing a company is alchemy—analyzing and distilling different elements into an entity with commercial value. The process is not a science but an art, and its practitioners—investment bankers—have to be creative thinkers. There is no absolute, right value for a company. Fortunately for von Sternberg, he understood the subjectiveness of the bankers' conclusions and suspected his company was worth considerably more. Although he eventually received a check for twice the amount the bankers thought Allen Corporation was worth, he didn't fault them. "That's what it was worth to them. Why does somebody pay $10,000 more for your house than someone else? Because it means more to them. They like the street or they like the school. Maybe the wife likes the breakfast nook. Things are worth more to different people. And we were worth a lot to Singer because we were a missing component of a grand master plan they had." Von Sternberg had sized up his buyer well.

Negotiations began in earnest after the meeting at the hotel. "I decided it wasn't enough," von Sternberg recalls, "and made a counteroffer for quite a bit more than what I'd settle for. The next meeting, they came back with a better offer. But most of the additional amount was based on an earn-out tied to the performance of the company. That wasn't completely acceptable, but we were getting close enough to get down to business. Most of the gamesmanship was on my part. Their first offer was really acceptable. I would have taken it if they had said, 'Take it or leave it.' But I felt I should get all that I could and asked for a lot more than I thought I could."

Seven months after negotiations began, von Sternberg and his attorney met with the Singer vice president and corporate attorney. The gigantic aerospace and sewing machine company laid out a new offer: $20 million cash for 100 percent of Allen Corp stock. Although the offer was the same amount proposed earlier, the earn-out clause had been removed. The offer contained two conditions: Von Sternberg and key executives had to sign two-year employment contracts and five-year noncompetes. To ensure that von Sternberg and the others stayed, Singer would put into escrow 10 percent of the purchase price and pay 9 percent interest. Half of the money would be released in a year and the other half after two years. In short, golden handcuffs.

Von Sternberg accepted on the spot. "It was a hell of an offer. We got 50-to-1 price earnings."

As von Sternberg shook hands with the new owner, the valuation experts from Geneva Corporation were still sifting through his books. When informed that the company had been sold, the bankers halted their accounting and refunded a portion of their fee.

## LAWYERS: LEGAL CHECKS

There are lawyers and there are lawyers. Sellers should consult attorneys with corporate acquisition and securities law experience rather than the garden-variety generalist. A lawyer should review every document that binds buyer and seller: letter of intent, purchase agreement, employment contract, noncompete. Everything.

Experienced lawyers do more than spot contractual loopholes. They ferret out potential obstacles to a sale hidden in a company pension plan, labor contract or debt covenant. If a buyer is a public company and offering stock, a lawyer advises the seller on insider restrictions, redemption rights, the pros and cons of common versus preferred stock, and SEC registration rights of any stock.

Lawyers are familiar with antitrust legislation and the provisions and guidelines of the Herfindahl-Hirschman Index, Clayton Act, Sherman Act, Federal Trade Commission Act, Robinson-Patman Act, Celler-Kefauver Act, Williams Act, Hart-Scott-Rodino Act and Department of Justice guidelines.

A seasoned acquisitions attorney knows if a federal agency, such as the Federal Communications Commission, Interstate Commerce Commission, Federal Aviation Administration, Federal Reserve Board or Comptroller of the Currency, must be notified and if a waiting period may delay a sale.

Lawyers are best at drafting and reviewing. They tend to the details that can be costly if overlooked, such as omissions of important facts, onerous employment contracts or seller claims that cannot be verified. They double-check tax ramifications, state laws about business transfers and whether a buyer has all the necessary documents.

In short, no sale should take place without an attorney. As invaluable as they are, though, attorneys should be kept in check. They should not be making business or commercial decisions. The seller decides what to sell, how to sell it and for how much. An attorney shows how to do it.

## ACCOUNTANTS: WEIGHING THE NUMBERS

"In starting another business, I would approach things differently. Number one, I would definitely get accounting help in the start-up, in setting up the books and giving financial advice. Even if it hurts a little, it's worth the money." —Shannon Edwards

In the world of acquisitions, mergers and sales, accountants are akin to the proverbial camel. They have poked their nose into the tent with their auditing and tax skills. By offering a variety of other services, they are now comfortably ensconced in the shelter. Accounting firms experienced in sales, such as the so-called Big Eight firms, have created separate consulting departments dedicated solely to acquisitions and sales.

Outside accountants are best equipped to help a company prepare for a sale—assemble financials, organize books, prepare financial statements and valuations, recast a financial history, and anticipate tax consequences of a sale. Since the 1986 Tax Act changed so much, a tax accountant is indispensable. New rules on how an installment sale or earn-out affects a seller's taxes and how to reduce or defer taxes require an accountant's reading. An accountant also helps a seller find the money to pay taxes and decide whether to apply to the IRS for a formal ruling on a transaction.

In an asset sale, especially with a large inventory, accountants help a seller establish the most advantageous accounting and valuation methods. Accounting methods, such as first-in, first-out and last-in, last-out valuation, can mean a big difference in a company's profits and purchase price. The experts with the calculators know whether inventory values should be recast for a sale and whether a company should alter its bookkeeping.

Accountants are familiar with how a buyer can record an acquisition on company books—as a purchase or a "pooling of interests"—and the implications of each and how these choices influence negotiations.

Fees for accountants are changing. Traditionally, the profession has barred contingency fees and instead toiled on an hourly basis. Most accountants still calculate fees on an hourly rate, especially for presale services such as audits and valuations. Nevertheless, although accountants usually don't charge contingency fees per se, their rates can vary depending on the size and complexity of a sale.

## APPRAISERS: COVERING YOUR ASSETS

**Appraisers** (sometimes called **business valuation experts**) offer a specialty within a specialty. Their expertise is valuation—determining the worth of assets. They're best used in establishing individual tax values among a basket of assets. After a sale, if the IRS challenges a company's valuation, appraisers are often hired to appear in tax court to substantiate asset values.

Over the years, the bread-and-butter business of appraisers has been valuing company assets for insurance, inheritance taxes or eminent domain transactions. They did the legwork to find out what a company's buildings, equipment and property were worth on the open market or if they had to be replaced. They are also used to value stock for a company with an Employee Stock Ownership Plan (ESOP).

Now business owners are asking appraisers to measure a company's tangible and intangible assets for possible sale. Owners without a lot of hard assets need to know the value of intangible assets—patents, software programs, trademarks, trade names, licenses, leases—that can constitute a significant portion of a selling price. Valuing intangibles is best done by an appraiser knowledgeable about the specific industry.

Appraisers generally use three valuation methods: cost, market and income. Cost is replacement value minus depreciation, market is its current commercial price, and income is how much a group of assets generates for a company.

Appraisers are unregulated. Anyone can use the title. They require no licensing or special schooling. However, professional associations such as the American Society of Appraisers have established educational and experience standards. Experience in acquisitions, expertise in an industry, success in tax cases and any accreditation are the best criteria for judging an assessor. Appraiser's fees vary greatly, ranging from an hourly rate to a flat fee for an entire job. A simple valuation can cost as little as $2,000, while complex assessments can run toward $50,000. The fee rises if an assessor must testify in tax court about a valuation.

## FOOLPROOF AGREEMENTS

Arrangements with your advisors are potentially troublesome. Misunderstandings, false assumptions and verbal disagreements about who's to do what and for how much arise easily. Misunderstandings also crop up around finders' fees. Imagine mentioning your plans to sell to a casual business acquaintance who later introduces you to your buyer. Do you owe your friend a finder's fee? Selling a company falls outside the normal course of business, so a person's role and responsibility must be defined for this special event.

Written agreements about roles, fees and communication requirements are essential. Even lawyers and accountants who have been on retainer for years should sign an "engagement letter" regarding fees and activities surrounding a sale. Acquisition lawyers and accountants may not sign anything more binding than a general description of services, hourly rates and billing cycles, arguing that they cannot know the entire scope and cost of their work until a sale is completed. So it is imperative that a seller monitor professional activities. Monitoring can head off duplicate efforts and "left-field" work. Costs can be kept in check through monthly billing, defined contingency arrangements and an established ceiling on fees.

The individual provisions of an agreement depend on circumstances and terms of the sale. A seller's best protection against excessive charges is defining roles, anticipating events and monitoring activities. What follows are points that should be considered in any agreement, although some items may not be applicable to a particular type of advisor. Think about the people involved in your sale, what can happen, and allow for contingencies.

### I. Description of Services

- Defined for an advisor assisting throughout the sale. If you use an attorney, investment banker and accountant, distinguish between their services. Specify which party should initiate and perform each task. Hold a coordination meeting to discuss roles and so avoid turf wars and wasted efforts.
- Narrowly defined individual assignments. These jobs may be finding and introducing qualified buyers, tax analysis, undertaking valuation, projecting future cash flow or earnings, preparing a selling memorandum, conducting an auction, assisting in negotiations, writing the purchase agreement, opinions and warranties.
- Assisting seller in determining schedules and deadlines.

### II. Fees and Commissions

- What is the basis for payment: percentage of selling price (cash price, stock value, notes, earn-outs, escrow deposits); flat fee, hourly or per diem rate; or percentage of buyer's or seller's stock? If stock, how will it be valued?
- Which out-of-pocket expenses such as air travel will be paid?
- If payment is an hourly fee, how often will seller be invoiced? How will invoices be itemized? Any cap on total fees? Are monthly statements expected?
- When are billings made? When is payment due? At closing, as work is performed or in installments?
- Who pays: seller, buyer, split by seller and buyer? If

seller, individual stockholders or the corporation? If a merger, the selling corporation or the surviving corporation?
- Can business broker or finder receive a fee from both buyer and seller?
- If seller is paying, where is the money to come from: sale of assets or sale of stock?
- Is fee dependent on completion of sale to any buyer? To buyer introduced directly or indirectly through broker or finder? To buyer found by the seller?
- Can officers or directors of selling company receive a finder's fee?

### III. Length of Time
- How long is the agreement in effect?
- Will fees be paid if a sale is made to a buyer introduced by finder but after the agreement has expired?

### IV. Type of Finder Agreement
- Exclusive, exclusive agency or nonexclusive?
- If exclusive, does finder receive a commission regardless of who introduces buyer to seller?
- If exclusive agency, does finder receive a commission even if seller locates buyer?
- If exclusive or exclusive agency, how long in effect?

### V. Protection of Confidential Information
- What information can be released to any prospective buyer?
- What information or documents must be kept confidential and disclosed only with seller's permission?
- Must finder provide name of potential buyer before seller releases information and signs nondisclosure agreement?
- Has seller required buyer to sign confidentiality agreement before releasing substantive information?

VI. **Amendments, Modifications, Cancellations and Extensions**
- Who can change the agreement and under what circumstances?
- Are oral changes acceptable?
- How can the agreement be canceled?
- If work is incomplete or sale incomplete and agreement is canceled, what fees will and will not be paid?

VII. **Indemnification:**  Service provider agrees that no other claim for fee or commission will be made on the seller.

VIII. **Signatures:**  Who signs the agreement—individual owner or all stockholders?

## ONE SELLER'S STORY: CIRCUS WORLD

Appraisers and lawyers played pivotal positions in the sale of a Florida theme park called Circus World. For owner Jim Monaghan, appraisers helped him decide which real estate to sell while lawyers almost unraveled the sale.

Monaghan is a fifty-year-old Phoenix businessman who has amassed a $70 million fortune trading real estate. When he bought Circus World it was sinking under a history of failure and a theme outdated by video games and science fiction movies. Yet it had value. The ninety-acre park was wrapped inside an 850-acre tract beside a busy interstate. Monaghan also saw a prize collection of Ferris wheels, rides and Western shows. "With increased attendance, it could be a money machine," he ventured.

Over two years, he phased out the big top attractions and replaced them with more exciting rides inspired by Germany's Oktoberfest. Attendance rose from 600,000 people a year to 1 million and gross revenues to $18 million. Then the money machine clanked to a halt.

When Monaghan bought Circus World, the liability insurance

premium cost $180,000 a year for a $25 million policy. The following year the insurance company reduced the policy to $1 million coverage and increased the premium to $750,000. Monaghan appealed to other insurance companies and even traveled to Lloyds of London looking for coverage. He recalls, "I was so annoyed that I refused to take any. It was a very bad mistake on my part because I was without it for about three or four months."

Eventually he found a way to limit the park's liability. He personally purchased at fair market value the land surrounding Circus World so that any claim against the park could not encompass the valuable real estate around it. "It was a way to protect myself," he explains. "I left a small area—a hundred acres—for the theme park. If I lost a suit I could say, 'The park is yours.' "

The insurance experience turned Monaghan against the theme park business. And those four unprotected months would come back to haunt him in a very expensive way.

With a mind to sell, he circulated within the theme park industry and attended a convention where he met the operators of Hershey Park and Six Flags. "There're only about five or six theme park operators in the country. If the price was right I knew one of these people would be interested in buying me out." Hershey Park was not interested, but Six Flags, a subsidiary of Bally Manufacturing Corporation, was eager to discuss a merger.

Monaghan had bought Circus World in 1984 from Mattel Toy Company for $10 million and increased its value. He borrowed $7 million to make improvements and almost doubled attendance. To determine the value of the land, he hired a real estate appraiser familiar with the local market. The appraiser spent a month researching titles and transactions involving similar plots, studying Monaghan's zoning applications, and calculating the value of future commercial development. Monaghan paid the appraiser $9,000 and received an estimated property value of $22 million.

Next he studied the theme park. "The value of the park is only good if it works, if it attracts money," Monaghan reasoned. "I looked at what I did to bring in a million people, then figured what someone like Six Flags could do. Also, these bigger operators can spread insurance among their parks and need only one national promotional budget. I did most of the numbers in my head, figuring how much I could push for, and it still looked like a good deal."

While talking with Six Flags, Monaghan received a phone call from the president of Cypress Gardens, another Florida resort park. He wanted to arrange a lunch with Monaghan and the chairman of Sea World Enterprises, a subsidiary of Harcourt Brace Jovanovich, Inc.

Monaghan and three HBJ men met in a suite at an Orlando hotel. The atmosphere was friendly and lunch was ordered. They waited until after eating to get down to business. Monaghan kicked off: "My attitude was, You want to buy me out—what are you prepared to offer?" The theme park executives responded: $8 million for an 80 percent interest. Monaghan's reaction was unequivocal: "That's ridiculous—I'm not interested. Why don't I pick up lunch and leave?" The buyer argued that Monaghan had paid that amount just two years earlier. Monaghan shot back, "I don't care what I paid for it, that's not what I'm selling it for." The meeting broke up with the Sea World men indicating they would be in touch.

Two weeks later the executives visited Circus World and walked around the park. Monaghan took them to lunch, and afterward the four reconvened in the HBJ headquarters in Orlando. A new offer was made. This time the proposal was in writing: a purchase agreement for 82 percent of Circus World based on a $15 million value. Monaghan countered, "No, but I will go to $18 million. If you scratch out what you've got, that's what we'll do." He also stipulated that HBJ assume Circus World's $7 million debt. The Sea World chairman ended the meeting by saying he would present Monaghan's proposal to the HBJ board of directors.

Two weeks passed before the Harcourt Brace Jovanovich board convened. Monaghan was in Hong Kong when he received a transoceanic telephone call. The Fortune 500 company had accepted his figure, but instead of buying 82 percent it wanted 100 percent ownership and would pay either cash or stock. The firm gave Monaghan one hour to make a decision. An experienced deal maker, Monaghan accepted the offer eight hours later.

To defer taxes, Monaghan opted for a stock swap. Because

the HBJ stock had been trading erratically, both sides agreed that its value would be fixed at a ten-day trading average starting eight days before closing. No maximum or minimum price was established, an oversight that would cost Monaghan dearly.

Closing day for Jim Monaghan began at the Harcourt Brace Jovanovich attorneys' offices at five o'clock in the afternoon. Twenty-one people, mostly lawyers, assembled to hammer out the final document. A major fear of the buyer was the four months that Circus World operated without liability insurance. "They were very concerned about the period I went naked," Monaghan recalls. "They were concerned about what would jump out of the closet. So they kept a considerably large holdout in escrow—$5 million —to cover any claims for two years."

Although Monaghan was selling only the ninety acres underneath Circus World, his plans for the surrounding real estate became entwined in the negotiations. The two sides went back and forth over road construction, zoning ordinances and Monaghan's intentions for a digital billboard along the highway. They debated operations, who would close Circus World during transition to the new owner and if the food caterer would stay. As the evening dragged out Monaghan's patience wore thin. He remembers, "It was the most horrendous, difficult deal I've ever done. On numerous occasions I left the room because I could not agree with their lawyers. They let their lawyers start to negotiate for them and their lawyers came close to having me walk away. The lawyers almost fucked up the deal—lawyers have a tendency to make a deal more difficult to justify their bullshit fees.

"Really, in truthfulness, I had nothing else going for me. I didn't have a written offer from Six Flags. I was gambling, playing a card game with them, and they were tough. Sometimes you get situations like that. You're not dealing with one Boone Pickens but with a group of people that all think they're hotshots. They probably looked at me and thought, Hey, this guy only paid $10 million. Why are we paying $18 million and picking up a debt of $7 million and he ends up with all the real estate? This guy is ripping us off. I knew full well that there were people on that team that didn't want that deal to fly."

Both sides pounded away, and by 3:45 a.m. they had an agreement. The only unfinished detail was the value of each share of HBJ stock, and a twist of fate and international politics would play a critical part. During the ten-day averaging period the United States retaliated against terrorism and bombed Libya. Public stockholders, guessing that tourists would be afraid to travel overseas and would stay home for vacations, ran up the prices of resort companies. Harcourt Brace Jovanovich stock bounced from the low 90s to more than 100 points. It later settled back, but that didn't help Monaghan. The ten-day trading average price for his stock was $99, even though on closing day HBJ stock was trading around $91. Monaghan says philosophically, "That was the deal I made. . . ."

[SAMPLE ENGAGEMENT LETTER]

(Date)

(Name and address of client)

_____

_____

Attention: _____

Gentlemen:

I am pleased to confirm our mutual understanding concerning the retention of Investment Banker, Inc., by (Name of Client—the "Company").

Investment Banker will assist the Company as its financial advisor and exclusive agent in connection with identifying and seeking out a person or group of persons satisfactory to the Company who would be interested in acquiring the stock or assets or acquiring through merger, consolidation or otherwise the Company (a "Business Combination") on terms that shall be satisfactory to the Company within its sole discretion. Such persons or group of persons are referred to herein as the "Prospective Purchasers." Investment Banker will review and analyze all indications of interest and proposals, both preliminary and firm, that are received, will advise the Company as to structure and valuation, and will assist the Company in negotiations with any Prospective Purchasers, whether or not identified by Investment Banker.

In connection with Investment Banker's activities on the Company's behalf, Investment Banker will, in conjunction with the Company's management, (a) develop a list of Prospective Purchasers and a strategy for the sale of the Company, (b) prepare a descriptive memorandum that describes the Company's operations, management and financial status and incorporates current financial data and other appropriate information furnished by the Company and (c) contact and elicit interest from Prospective Purchasers.

In connection with Investment Banker's activities on the Company's behalf, the Company will furnish Investment Banker with all information concerning the Company (the "Information") that Investment Banker reasonably deems appropriate.

The Company represents and warrants that all Information made available to Investment Banker by the Company will be complete and correct in all material respects and will not contain any untrue statements of a material fact or omit to state a material fact necessary in order to make the statements therein not misleading in light of the circumstances under which such statements are made. In rendering its services hereunder, including the preparation of the memorandum referred to above, Investment Banker will be using and relying primarily on the Information without independent verification thereof or independent appraisal of any of the Company's assets. Further, in evaluating other companies, Investment Banker will be using information contained in public reports and possibly other information furnished to Investment Banker by such other companies. In connection with its evaluation of other companies, Investment Banker will use its best efforts to provide the Company with information concerning such other companies that is complete and correct in all material respects; notwithstanding the foregoing, Investment Banker does not assume responsibility for the accuracy or completeness of the Information or information regarding such other companies.

In order to coordinate efforts to effect a transaction satisfac-

tory to the Company, during the period of the engagement of
Investment Banker hereunder, neither the Company nor its management or representatives will initiate any contacts or discussions with any Prospective Purchasers, except through or together
with Investment Banker, the Company will inform Investment
Banker of any contacts made by it or on its behalf with any Prospective Purchasers (including any who were not identified and
contacted by Investment Banker), and the Company will keep
Investment Banker timely informed of any developments or negotiations with any Prospective Purchasers. In the event that
during the period of the engagement of Investment Banker hereunder the Company or its management or representatives is (are)
contacted by or on behalf of a Prospective Purchaser concerning
the possibility of the acquisition of the Company or its stock or
assets which the Company's management believes merits further
consideration, the Company will promptly so inform Investment
Banker in order that Investment Banker can evaluate such Prospective Purchaser and its interest and assist the Company, including in any subsequent discussions.

Upon the execution of this agreement you shall pay $_____
to Investment Banker as a nonreturnable fee for its services under
this agreement. Such amount shall be a credit against and de-
ducted from the additional fee payable to Investment Banker if
there is a Business Combination as provided below:

If a Business Combination occurs involving the Company,
whether in whole or part, in one or a series of transactions, then
the Company will pay Investment Banker a fee in cash on closing
according to the following formula, less the $_____ paid to In-
vestment Banker upon the execution of this agreement: __ % of
the first $_____ of consideration paid or payable; plus __ % of all
consideration paid or payable in excess of $_____.

The consideration received for this purpose (regardless of
whether the Business Combination is in the form of an asset sale,
stock sale, merger, consolidation or other form of transaction)
shall be the aggregate consideration paid for the stock or assets
of the Company. If the consideration paid is other than cash, the
consideration shall be the fair market value thereof.

Notwithstanding the above, if the consideration payable in

connection with the transaction includes contingent future payments, the Company agrees to pay Investment Banker a fee determined in accordance with the two immediately preceding paragraphs as, when and if said contingency payments are received. However, in the event of an installment purchase at a fixed price and a fixed time schedule, the Company agrees to pay Investment Banker at the time of the closing a fee determined in accordance with the two immediately preceding paragraphs discounted according to the Treasury note rate corresponding to the scheduled deferred/installment payment dates. As used in this agreement the term "consideration" shall not include compensation for employment, consulting or other personal services equal to that amount paid during the last calendar year. Any compensation paid above that amount shall be treated as "consideration" in determining the fee payable to Investment Banker.

The term of this agreement shall be *one year* from the date of your signing and thereby confirming your acceptance of the provisions of this letter, unless earlier terminated as hereinafter provided. Investment Banker shall be entitled to the additional percentage fee described above for any Business Combination with a Prospective Purchaser, if such Prospective Purchaser was introduced and/or contacted by Investment Banker, the Company or any other party during the period in which this agreement was in effect, and the transaction is consummated within *two years* after the termination of this agreement.

The Company agrees to reimburse Investment Banker, upon request from time to time, for all reasonable out-of-pocket expenses incurred (including fees and disbursements of counsel, if required) in connection with Investment Banker acting for the Company pursuant to this agreement.

In consideration of the agreement of Investment Banker to act on the Company's behalf pursuant to this agreement, the Company agrees to indemnify and hold harmless Investment Banker and its affiliates, the respective partners, directors, officers, agents, employees (and their legal representatives) of Investment Banker and its affiliates and each person, if any, controlling Investment Banker or any of its affiliates within the meaning of either Section 15 of the Securities Act of 1933 or Section 20 of the Securities

Exchange Act of 1934 from and against any and all losses, claims, damages and liabilities, joint or several (and all actions in respect thereof), caused by, related to or arising out of Investment Banker acting for the Company pursuant to this agreement, and to reimburse Investment Banker and any other person entitled to be indemnified hereunder for all expenses (including reasonable fees and disbursements of legal counsel) as they are incurred in connection with investigating, preparing or defending such action or claim, whether or not in connection with pending or threatened litigation in which Investment Banker or any other indemnified person is a party or threatened to be made a party; provided, however, that the Company will not be liable under this paragraph to the extent that any loss, claim, damage, liability or expense results from gross negligence or wilful misconduct of Investment Banker. These indemnification and expense reimbursement provisions are in addition to any liability that the Company might otherwise have to Investment Banker or to any other person. The Company also agrees that neither Investment Banker nor any of its affiliates, nor any partner, director, officer, agent, employee (or their legal representatives) of Investment Banker or any of its affiliates nor any person controlling Investment Banker or any of its affiliates (as described above), shall have any liability (whether direct or indirect, in contract or tort or otherwise) to the Company for or in connection with the engagement of Investment Banker, except for any such liability for losses, claims, damages, liabilities or expenses that is found in a final judgment to have resulted primarily from gross negligence or wilful misconduct of Investment Banker.

In order to provide for just and equitable contribution, if (a) a claim for indemnification pursuant to this agreement is made but it is found in a final judicial determination, not subject to further appeal, that such indemnification may not be enforced in such case, even though the express provisions of this agreement provide for indemnification in such case, or (b) contribution under the federal securities laws or otherwise may be sought with respect to the matters covered by the foregoing indemnity, then the Company, on the one hand, and Investment Banker, on the other hand, shall contribute to the losses, claims, damages, liabilities or expenses to which they may be subject in either such case in such proportions so that Investment Banker is responsible in the agreement for such a percentage of such losses, claims, damages, liabilities or expenses equal to a fraction, the numerator of which is the amount of the fees received by Investment Banker pursuant to this agreement and the denominator of which is the aggregate consideration to be received in the Business Combination, and the Company shall be responsible for the remainder of such losses, claims, damages, liabilities or expenses; provided, however, that if such allocation is not permitted by applicable law, then the relative fault of the Company, on the one hand, and Investment Banker, on the other hand, in connection with the statements or omissions that resulted in such losses, claims, damages, liabilities or expenses and other relevant equitable considerations shall also be considered. No person found liable for a fraudulent misrepresentation shall be entitled to contribution from any person who is not also found liable for such fraudulent misrepresentation. Notwithstanding the foregoing, Investment Banker shall not be obliged to contribute any amount hereunder that exceeds the amount of fees Investment Banker receives pursuant to this agreement. If the full amount of contribution specified in this paragraph is not permitted by law, then the party seeking contribution shall be entitled to contribution hereunder to the full extent of such contribution permitted by law.

Investment Banker agrees to notify the Company promptly of the assertion against Investment Banker of any claim or the commencement of any action or proceeding relating to the services rendered pursuant to this agreement, but such failure to so notify the Company shall not relieve the Company from any obligation or liability that the Company may have pursuant to this letter to the extent that the Company has not been prejudiced in any material respect by such failure. Investment Banker shall have the right to retain counsel of its own choice to represent Investment Banker and such counsel shall, to the fullest extent consistent with its professional responsibilities, cooperate with the Company and any counsel designated by the Company. The Company shall not be liable under this agreement for any settlement of any claim, action or proceeding against Investment Banker or any other indemnified person identified hereunder made without the Company's written consent, which consent will not be unreasonably withheld.

Either party hereto may terminate this agreement at any time upon 30 days prior written notice, without liability or continuing obligation to Investment Banker or to the Company (except for any compensation earned by Investment Banker up to the date of termination), except as set forth in the following sentence. Neither termination nor completion of the engagement or services of Investment Banker pursuant to this agreement shall affect the indemnification provisions of this agreement (or any other provisions intended to survive such termination or completion), which provisions shall remain operative and in full force and effect following such termination or completion.

The validity and interpretation of this agreement shall be governed by the law of the State of _____ applicable to agreements made and to be fully performed therein.

The benefits of this agreement shall inure to the respective successors and assigns of the parties hereto and of the indemnified persons hereunder and their successors and assigns and other legal representatives, and the obligations and liabilities assumed in this agreement by the parties hereto shall be binding upon their respective successors and assigns. Notwithstanding the foregoing, neither party may assign its rights and obligations hereunder without the consent of the other party.

If the foregoing correctly sets forth our agreement, please sign the enclosed copy of this letter in the space provided and return it to us.

Yours very truly,
INVESTMENT BANKER, INC.

By: _____

(Managing Director)

Confirmed and agreed to:
This _____ day of _____, 1987
(Name of client)

By: _____

| CHAPTER | WHAT'S YOUR |
|:---:|:---:|
| 4 | COMPANY WORTH? |

"What's my company worth?" is most sellers' first question. The answer can be elusive. People use different techniques. While accountants and valuation experts apply formulas and equations, sellers often rely on experience and gut instinct. Entire books have been written about valuation—how to figure what a company is worth. For most, it's the heart and soul of the sale process.

We offer here basic valuation methods. These are helpful for private companies with no publicly traded stock and with income statements and balance sheets designed mainly for internal use or tax returns. Their private nature makes valuation less cut-and-dried and more a scrambling together of theoretical numbers with a splash of intuition.

The first thing to keep in mind is the difference between value and price. They're not the same. Value is an internal figure—a dollar amount representing the sum total of a company. Everything in a company affects its value—hard assets, debts, earnings, growth, management, market share, competitive position, technology. Nevertheless, value may be in the eyes of the beholder. If two buyers want a company badly, one buyer may pay far in excess of value. On the other hand, a shareholder dispute or a cash flow crunch may result in a sale way below value.

Price is an external figure. It's what outsiders, whether they be 100 percent buyers, the stock market or minority investors, are

willing to pay in today's market. Price is more subjective than
value. It can be moved by egos, popularity, fads and even whim.

A seller determines both the company's value and price range
in today's market before talking to a buyer. No one wants to begin
negotiations with the blind query, "What's it worth to you?" A
seller knows its worth and has priced the company *beforehand*.

## FOUR METHODS, NO ABSOLUTES

> "I sold kind of the tail end of my business. I basically gave it away for
> just 10 percent of what it would have taken in over the next year. Just
> to make sure the clients would be taken care of. To me that's better
> than closing the doors. That does so much damage to the image of small
> business. One day just disappearing. Your phone's disconnected, and
> clients have no place for services or to buy products."—Dee Weitzel

A company can be valued four ways, although some people may
combine methods or refine them. Applied to the same company,
each method produces a different total. This suggests—no,
confirms—that no single number equals the value of a company.
Formulas or methods should be used as rough gauges, not precise
calipers.

### #1. PRICE/EARNINGS AND OTHER RATIOS

A company's financial operations can be stated in financial ratios
that reveal something about its health. As a valuation tool, a selling
company's ratios are compared with ratios of similar companies
(same industry, size and financial history) that have been sold.
(Average industry ratios are published in the U.S. Bureau of Census
*Quarterly Financial Report for Manufacturing, Mining and Trade
Corporations* and by Dun & Bradstreet.) A company estimates its
value by comparing ratios with those of comparable companies.

The most common ratio is **price to earnings, or P/E**, which
is a measurement of a company's earning power. It expresses a
company value as a multiple of net after-tax earnings. For instance,

a company earning $500,000 a year that is comparable with a company selling for a P/E of 7 to 10 values itself between $3.5 million and $5 million. It figures thus:

$500,000 (earnings) × P/E 7  = $3,500,000 (price)
$500,000 (earnings) × P/E 10 = $5,000,000 (price)

A private company can use P/E to compare itself with a publicly traded company whose P/E is reported in the newspaper. The public company's selling price is its quoted stock price, and its earnings are quarterly results. A seller with a company generating strong earnings growth attaches a higher P/E to its value.

Earnings can be adjusted, however, as any accounting student knows. Generally accepted accounting principles allow companies different ways of financial reporting. Earnings are affected by how and when a company recognizes income and expenses; how and when it values inventory; how it accounts for bad debts; how it values intangible assets; what its depreciation methods are; how it treats investment tax credits; and how it handles tax losses. Any comparison of P/E ratios should encompass a comparison or adjustment of earnings calculations. Otherwise, comparing P/E multiples is an apples and oranges mismatch.

Other financial ratios enhance or reduce a company's P/E valuation. The **return on sales** ratio compares total sales to net income and indicates how much a company is making on each sales dollar. The higher a company's margin, the greater its value. If the margin exceeds the industry average a seller should try to increase the P/E or add a premium to the company value.

Here's how to determine profit margin:

$$\frac{\$100,000 \text{ (net income)}}{\$500,000 \text{ (total sales)}} = 20 \text{ percent}$$

The **return on equity** and **return on assets** (also called **return on investment**) ratios are similar and are often used by experienced buyers. These ratios measure a company's profitability by comparing net income with equity or total assets. If ratios are higher than those of other companies in the same industry, the company being valued is worth more. As with the return on sales ratio, high return on equity or return on assets can justify a high P/E value.

Here's how to determine these ratios:

$$\frac{\$100,000 \text{ (net income)}}{\$750,000 \text{ (equity or net worth)}} = 13.3 \text{ percent return on equity}$$

$$\frac{\$100,000 \text{ (net income)}}{\$700,000 \text{ (total assets)}} = 14.2 \text{ percent return on assets}$$

Earnings valuations have two limitations. First, a company has to have demonstrable earnings. Second, these valuations are based on the idea that companies can be compared and sold at similar prices. It makes few allowances for a company that doesn't fit an industry mold or whose operations or history do not follow others.

## ONE SELLER'S STORY: Computer Power Systems Corporation

A combination of ratios, formulas and even personal emotion may be used in valuation. In the case of Los Angeles-based Computer Power Systems Corporation, three groups of people—shareholders, venture capitalists and investment bankers—relied on different methods. In the end, the investment bankers prevailed. But the real winner was the seller who, as a result of putting the company through a rigorous valuation, received more for its company than it expected.

Computer Power Systems, the brainchild of William Lennartz and two partners, designs and manufactures wiring systems to regulate the electrical flow for large computer users. A hybrid between electrical manufacturing and the computer service industry, the company quickly found a niche securing customers among such Fortune 500 companies as Rockwell International and Burroughs Corp. By 1984, eight years after Lennartz launched it, Computer Power Systems logged sales around $20 million and pretax earnings around $1 million. Despite its rapid growth Lennartz decided to sell.

"We wanted to find a strong financial partner that would have selling and market muscle," Lennartz says. As the major stockholder, he adds a more compelling reason. "The real goal was to get liquid personally. To convert my stock in a small, undercapitalized, privately held company, whose certificates I couldn't do anything with, into cash."

When the board of directors agreed to seek a buyer it also enlisted the services of an investment banking firm. One of the directors knew someone in the Los Angeles office of Lehman Brothers, so that firm was hired. (Their $350,000 fee was based partly on the price.) As the investment bankers prepared a sales document and valuation, the board wrestled with its own valuation.

The board was composed of two groups—individual stockholders and venture capitalists. For the stockholders, valuation was an emotional response, a gut reaction. "It basically had to do with the minimum price we would accept," explains Lennartz. "It was a personal decision. You say to yourself, Would I take $7 a share? And either you feel comfortable with that or not. If you're desperate you'd take anything. If not . . . ." On the other side of the table were venture capitalists who held 35 percent of company stock. They insisted on a specific return on investment: tripling their original $1.5 million investment in three years or quintupling it in five years.

The investment goals of the venture capitalists shaped the board's thinking. "What it really came down to was satisfying the venture capitalists on a return that was worth it to them," Lennartz says. "Once we got them satisfied, all the major shareholders were satisfied with taking that price." The board settled on $9 million for the value of Computer Power Systems.

The investment bankers were sailing on a different tack. Lennartz describes their process: "Lehman took a look at the company, its goodwill, the future earnings ability, and, based on future sales projections and future earnings, determined the value. They thought our number was much too low and they could ask for a price that was twice our minimum valuation. They based this on future earnings, a five-year profit-and-loss projection. We were in a high growth market and in a leadership position." Lehman Brothers valued Computer Power Systems at $17 million.

To find a buyer, Lennartz and Lehman Brothers compiled a

list of fifty potential targets—companies in the industry, customers, known acquirers. From the list of fifty they selected five to receive the sales document. This was a package describing Computer Power Systems' history, financial record, market share, competitors and future. They limited the first mailing to five because, says Lennartz, "We didn't want to shop the thing." He knew that a company picked over by the general market does not get top dollar.

Two weeks later one of the five, Emerson Electric Company, a $1.2 billion electronics firm headquartered in St. Louis, visited Computer Power Systems. One week later they called Lehman Brothers to signal their strong interest and ask for an exclusive look of the company. Lennartz explains: "They didn't want to get into a bidding war. They didn't want to spend a month doing due diligence, then find out we were selling to GE. And they didn't want to give us a bid that we would take to someone else, like GE, then back to them for more."

Lehman Brothers informed Emerson that the only way to eliminate other potential buyers was to make a preemptive bid—an offer high enough to justify undivided attention. Emerson arranged for another inspection of the southern California facility before it took the plunge.

Lennartz describes what happened: "We went into my office —just me, the Emerson group vice president and the Lehman partner. The Emerson guy right off says they're very interested in the company but that the price was way too high at $17 million. They thought it was ridiculous. So the Lehman fellow asks, 'Well, what do you have in mind?' And Emerson said it could see paying $12 million. Right there I'm about to come out of my chair to shake their hands and say, 'Done. Let me call my wife!'

"But the Lehman guy says, 'That sounds about as ridiculous to us as maybe our $17 million sounds to you. How about somewhere in between?' So the V.P. said, 'We can go as high as $13.5, but that's our maximum.' And the Lehman fellow says it's in the low end of our ballpark and we'll have to talk to our shareholders. But on the basis of that offer we'll call everybody else off and give Emerson sixty days to do due diligence and come up with an agreement we're all happy with." After five minutes of negotiation Computer Power Systems had a buyer.

The three agreed that five Computer Power Systems executives would sign two-year employment contracts. Also, $1.5 million of the purchase price would be placed in escrow for one year to cover uncollected receivables and representations and warranties made about the condition of assets and liabilities.

When due diligence uncovered nothing to derail the sale, lawyers started drafting the purchase agreement before Emerson auditors finished. Seeing Emerson as eager as he to complete the process, Lennartz was sanguine about the deal. While he had to ride herd on the lawyers, sometimes calling them daily to ensure they were doing all the necessary legal work, he was pleased. He liked Emerson and the way it bargained in good faith without attempting to alter their agreement.

Closing day, says Lennartz, "was one of the most exciting moments of my life. Unfortunately, it only lasted five or ten minutes. Then it was horribly anticlimactic." He flew to St. Louis and joined his buyers in a large conference room in the offices of Emerson attorneys. The room was dotted with piles of documents. For two hours Lennartz signed his name hundreds of times.

Unlike some founders, Lennartz has no hesitations or regrets: "We had found a great corporate partner and were getting more for the company than we first agreed. I was converting a major part of my personal net worth into cash and was excited to no end." The atmosphere was relaxed. Someone joked about Lennartz traveling with a handful of multimillion-dollar cashier checks for the other stockholders back in L.A. It was Friday afternoon. Lennartz boarded the one o'clock plane to return home for a celebratory dinner and an eight-week sabbatical.

#### #2. BACK TO THE FUTURE

This method, called **discounted present value of future cash flow,** values a company according to how much cash or earnings it will produce in the future. It anticipates what a company will earn tomorrow to establish its value today. It estimates cash that a company should generate in the future, then discounts those dollars to present-day values. This valuation is based on two predictions: how much cash or earnings a company will produce and future interest rates.

While the term sounds complicated and contradictory (like "Back to the Future"), the concept is simple. It works thus: a seller estimates future earnings or cash flow over a select number of years (for instance, five), then discounts or reduces these dollars to eliminate their growth due to interest rates. The discounted earnings total is added to a "residual" value. This represents a company's worth beyond the period used in figuring future earnings. It's subjectively chosen to represent what the company will be worth at the end of the period for which cash flows are measured.

This method is rife with assumptions and estimates. The first conjecture arises in figuring the revenues and expenses that will constitute future earnings or cash and the years they will cover. The next variable is the **discount ratio**—who knows what is going to happen to interest rates or the value of money in the 1990s? (Insurance companies and business publishers issue schedules and tables showing changing dollar values based on future interest rates. But these are estimates, not predictions.) Estimating the residual value of a company beyond the immediate future is serious crystal-ball gazing.

Here's a simplified example of how this method works. Let's say a company will earn, based on past performance, $500,000 over the next five years and the projected average annual interest rate is 12 percent. Its discounted present value looks like this:

|        | EARNINGS/CASH | DISCOUNTED BY 12% |
|--------|---------------|-------------------|
| Year 1 | $100,000      | $89,290 (at end of year) |
| Year 2 | $100,000      | $79,720           |
| Year 3 | $100,000      | $71,180           |
| Year 4 | $100,000      | $63,550           |
| Year 5 | $100,000      | $56,740           |

Total discounted earnings: $360,480
Residual value: $200,000
Total value: $560,480

### #3. GROSS REVENUE BASIS

Some companies are cash cows. They generate large streams of income and matching expenses. They often have few assets, little capital investment and meager, if any, retained earnings. They're consulting firms, radio stations, temporary service or employment agencies, public relations or advertising companies, professional services businesses, insurance brokerage companies, retail establishments or dealerships. These can be valued by annual gross revenues.

A company's value is expressed as a multiple of annual gross revenues. Different multiples are applied to different kinds of businesses. Multiples start below 1 (insurance brokerage companies are purportedly valued at 80 percent of gross revenues) and rise into the teens and beyond. The multiple depends on both objective and subjective factors. These include how long a company has been producing revenues and their dependability (revenues produced by offering discounts or premiums are less valuable), and a company's reputation, the quality of its sales force, and whether its industry is popular among buyers. Buying fads affect multiples. Companies in demand, whether computer software designers or advertising agencies, command a higher multiple because of their popularity.

Establishing a multiple requires research and guesswork. Research finds what similar companies have sold for. Good sources for this information are industry associations and news accounts of recent sales. Guesswork comes in judging whether revenues are dependable and whether they will continue to match or exceed the benchmark level.

Here's a simple example of how this method works: A public relations company with a seven-year history of revenues fluctuating between $280,000 and $910,000 (gross revenues before expenses or taxes) chooses a three-year period with average revenues of $750,000. Similar firms are selling at 1.5 multiple, but the seller demonstrates stronger sales. Consequently, the seller estimates that the company is worth two times revenues and fixes its value at $1.5 million.

One variable in this method is the specific year or period

chosen as the benchmark. This choice is critical for a company whose revenues do not follow a clear pattern or cycle. It's debatable which year represents a company's true performance. Any year a seller chooses has to be explained and justified.

Another approach applies a multiple to estimated future gross earnings. This is useful for companies with lackluster revenues but on the edge of a revenue spurt. Companies about to launch a new product or hire a super salesperson, and likely to produce much higher gross revenues, can use this method. Instead of using past revenues, a seller adds up estimated future revenues over a number of years, then adjusts this figure to present-day dollars. This adjustment is made by reducing future revenues by estimated future interest rates, say 15 percent, to arrive at the value of present dollars. The calculations are the same as those for discounted present value of future cash flow.

## ONE SELLER'S STORY: Station WEBN

Frank Wood, a forty-three-year-old Cincinnati businessman, made it his business to know how to value radio stations. He says, "Broadcast properties change hands on a multiple of cash flow, 'cash flow' being defined as operating profit before depreciation, amortization or interest. That's a hard-and-fast figure. But the question is then, 'What's the multiple?' "

A restless deal maker with a law degree and a desire to be "one of the majors," Wood was always on the lookout to acquire radio properties. His springboard—Station WEBN Cincinnati, an irreverent, flamboyant FM rock-and-roll station he and his father put on the air in 1967—sounds like the prototype for the television sitcom *WKRP in Cincinnati.*

As WEBN grew in listenership and revenues, it became the target of media buyers. "It was a wholly owned property and there aren't very many of them," Wood recounts. "A lot of people would circle like sharks, thinking they'd find hay in your hair." No hayseed, Wood hung on to his station and explored ways to expand. In 1980, he acquired a flagging Louisville station that he hoped to turn around.

"I was at a stage in life with two very successful radio properties with some debt, but cash flowing beautifully," he relates. "I could take out any amount of money or buy another station and then another one all by the time I was fifty. I could have three or four stations. That would keep me in a small arena. Or I could do it another way. I could get into a faster lane, a bigger arena, and make a pile of money, only I wouldn't own as much of it." When Jacor Communications Inc., a Cincinnati-based public owner of eleven radio stations, approached Wood he was ready to listen. Selling to Jacor, Wood concluded, "was not only a way to take advantage of a favorable market but a backdoor way of taking WEBN public. I could have my cake and eat it, too."

Wood didn't want to retire or sell out; he wanted to move up. The Jacor proposal of stock and a managerial position neatly fit his plans. Wood and the Jacor chairman met to explore the sale of WEBN at a Cincinnati country club. "I need to find out more about Jacor," Wood told him. "I want to take a lot of your stock so I want to know more about your financial underpinnings." Wood requested copies of Jacor's registration statements filed with the Securities and Exchange Commission and annual report. He also obtained a profit-and-loss statement on each Jacor property.

In turn, Jacor wanted the inside picture on WEBN and its profit-and-loss statement. Wood was prepared. "That had to be reconstructed," he says about refiguring his bottom line. "The bookkeeper and I did it. I had a Big Eight accounting firm for taxes, but we did the review reconstruction. It wasn't brain surgery. I knew how a public or new company would operate and how much 'family effect' there was. I did have to figure out things like my salary and what someone else would pay a general manager."

The two chief executives advanced to more intricate negotiations. Wood knew from experience that WEBN's value lay in its cash flow, not profits. "Retained earnings weren't very high," he says. "The thing had a theoretical negative net worth, which is very common in broadcast companies because you don't have many assets. The overwhelming value is the value of the franchise, which goes up and up, and is a non-balance sheet item until you sell it. Ours wasn't a very impressive balance sheet—no radio property is."

The pivotal point in valuing WEBN was the multiple, and in

late 1985 radio stations were hot. "I was looking at other broadcast deals and the multiple danced around," Wood remembers. "There was a feeding frenzy for all kinds of media properties. The prices were just crazy and the multiple kept going up—7, 8, 10. Some traded hands at 11. As interest rates dropped multiples climbed." Wood and the Jacor chairman fixed on a multiple between 8 and 9.

Next Wood had to select the year for the basis of the cash flow total. He chose 1985 even though he had to estimate revenues for November and December. In hindsight, he wishes he had picked another year. "If I had held on another eight or nine months I might have gotten a higher price because the station had a better cash flow. And I could have made the operations look better—not spend any money on promotion, things like that. But I thought that was shortsighted. I loved the radio property. It was like my first kid. I really didn't want to sell EBN outright." Revenues for the year were $3.6 million, with an operating profit between $1.4 million and $1.5 million.

At the second meeting Wood and Jacor arrived at a multiple and a price. Wood says, "We agreed on a $12 million price. I wanted a million shares of stock—about 10 percent of their outstanding shares. It was selling right then around $4. And $8 million in cash." [Wood wanted cash to pay off debts and past taxes even though he would have deferred taxes from the sale if he had received most of the purchase price in voting stock.]

"The money was the easy part. We argued about what my title was going to be and the board of directors. I wanted a seat and the right to nominate another director. Initially they offered me executive vice president and no seat on the board. I said, 'No thank you,' and walked. It was a deal breaker for me."

A week later the Jacor chairman invited Wood to meet the Jacor board of directors. This time they offered him president and chief executive officer but still haggled over board seats. A face-saving compromise broke the deadlock: Jacor would give Wood his seat on the board as well as the nomination of a new member, but subject to the approval of the existing board.

Ironically, Wood did not insist on his new position in writing. "I told them, 'I don't need an employment contract and you don't need a noncompete from me. I'll work here as long as I like it and as long as you guys like it.' I can walk out of here anytime I want. If they fire me I have a 'put' on my stock written into the sale agreement. If I quit I have a different kind of 'put' on my stock. I wanted to protect myself from getting whipsawed, and they, of course, wanted to protect themselves from me doing something strange."

Final negotiations for the sale of Station WEBN were completed around Christmas, but both parties, especially Wood, preferred to keep it quiet. "I didn't want to announce it until it had been reduced to a binding contract, and that wasn't signed until late January. Then the stock jumped 50 percent. And I thought, Hey, this is a lot of fun. Now I'm on a faster track and hitting my stride."

## #4. ASSET VALUATION

"I would have personally owned the real estate in the company. Corporations don't buy companies because they want real estate assets. Corporations buy because they want the earnings power. If I own real estate I can separate it from the sale and lease it back to the new owner."
—Bill Lennartz

Most businesses are valued on a **going concern** basis that assumes they will continue to sell services or products, generate income and produce a profit. One method of valuation, however, can be applied to a company on the brink of bankruptcy. Asset valuation is also useful for a company whose individual assets are more valuable than the company as a whole and when a buyer wants to liquidate. An aging manufacturing plant sitting on valuable real estate would fall into this category.

This valuation produces a rock-bottom value, the very least a seller would accept. Any company on the ropes should value its assets before looking for a sale. Of course, asset valuation has to include subtracting liabilities.

Asset valuation assigns an amount to every tangible and intangible asset. It sounds simple, but a tangible asset can be valued in two ways—historical or cost value, or fair market value. Sometimes neither method seems adequate, for instance for film or photo libraries, raw land on the edge of development, long-term leases or loans at favorable rates. For some assets, there is no handy "bluebook" listing their measurable value—their value is a coin toss. A professional appraiser is useful in these valuations.

Total company assets (if they aren't mainly fixed or intangible assets) can be valued by applying the **current** or **quick ratios**. These indicate a company's ability to pay off short-term debt and show liquidity. As with other ratios, these are compared with an industry average. An above-average performance justifies adding a premium to a company's book value.

For the current ratio, current assets are divided by current liabilities; for the quick ratio, current assets minus inventory (considered the least liquid asset as are certain prepaids like insurance premiums) are divided by current liabilities. Here are the formulas:

$$\frac{\$500,000 \,(\text{current assets})}{\$100,000 \,(\text{current liabilities})} = 5 \text{ times}$$

$$\frac{\$350,000 \,(\text{current assets} - \text{inventory and prepaids})}{\$100,000 \,(\text{current liabilities})} = 3.5 \text{ times}$$

Asset valuation gets tricky when putting a figure on *intangibles* such as client lists, distribution networks, contracts, market share, patents, copyrights, trademarks, software, leases, government permits, transportation systems, exclusive access to natural resources and exceptional employees. There is no hard-and-fast value for many intangibles, so a seller assigns a value based on the best available information, such as sales of similar assets.

A seller may add another intangible to the list of assets: *goodwill*. Goodwill, sometimes called **going business value**, is a company's reputation with customers, clients and in the marketplace. The IRS, in Revenue Ruling 59–60, defines goodwill more broadly: "The presence of goodwill and its value, therefore, rests on the excess over and above the fair return on the net tangible assets."

Goodwill is a controversial item in many sales. Although it is an elusive intangible, most sellers believe they should receive some payment for goodwill. On the other hand, buyers resist purchasing goodwill for tax and accounting reasons. Unlike other assets, goodwill cannot be amortized and depreciated, because its useful life cannot be determined. So it sits like a lump in the buyer's books, never to produce tax deductions like other assets.

A seller seeking to increase company value with goodwill should be prepared to haggle. A seller's chances of convincing a buyer to pay for goodwill are improved by a clear valuation system. Because goodwill is based largely on earnings power, excess future earnings can be projected and measured. Although this job should be left to accountants, it is essentially a process of subtraction. If a company's total value exceeds the value of its liquidated net assets, the difference is goodwill. Put another way, goodwill is any portion of a company's value over and above the fair market value of its other assets—tangible, intangible and net working capital such as cash, accounts receivable and inventory.

## ONE SELLER'S STORY: *Roll Call*

A venerable tabloid published for thirty-two years on Capitol Hill, *Roll Call* had lots of goodwill and little else. A folksy publication that easily and equally covered congressional birthdays and congressional committees, it boasted 7,000 readers (half unpaid). But more important, it had the reputation for being the house organ of the U.S. Congress. *Roll Call*, despite its cursory coverage, occupied a special niche among members of Congress and their staffs. Nonetheless, the paper always seemed to operate on a shoestring. Owner Sidney Yudain served as editor and publisher of this sole proprietorship, and kept staff to a minimum.

Undoubtedly, its unique position on Capitol Hill accounted for the steady stream of would-be buyers. Yudain says he was constantly approached and routinely turned down all offers to sell until fall 1985. Then he began to listen. "When you have a baby you never really want consciously to cut the strings. But I was resigned to selling the paper because I had had it. I thought it was time. If something happened to me there wouldn't be any paper.

The years of building would have gone down the drain and it would have been worth nothing. A lot of reasoning went into it. Congress was changing, I had been through thirty years of it. . . ."

He abruptly broke off talks with one buyer because it was unqualified: "It turned out to be a facetious offer. They didn't have the money. Didn't understand what the paper was all about. Didn't understand the value. Their offer was nowhere near what I was asking."

Yudain established the value of *Roll Call* by weighing its tangibles and intangibles. He had never incorporated so he had only assets to sell. While revenues were modest—$150,000 to $175,000 a year—and assets were limited to used office furniture and equipment, Yudain put great value on the paper's name. "My value was probably arbitrary, but it was based on the importance of the paper, the uniqueness, its position in the community. And the fact that we were generating national advertising. I had received an offer in 1964—$250,000 for 49 percent. At the time I figured it was worth at least half a million or more. So here it was twenty years later and I placed the value at $750,000."

The next seeker was the *National Journal*, another Washington, D.C., publication, which covered not only Capitol Hill but also the executive and judicial branches of government. But talks between the two parties floundered. Meanwhile Yudain was asked to lunch by Arthur Levitt, Jr., chairman of the American Stock Exchange and head of the newly created Levitt Communications. Levitt was eager to acquire a publication and wanted *Roll Call*.

Although hesitant to open negotiations, not because of the *National Journal* but because he was leaving for the Virgin Islands the next morning, Yudain told Levitt his asking price. As it turned out they didn't negotiate. Levitt simply put a counteroffer on the table: $500,000 cash for 90 percent of the paper. Feeling the amount was close enough, Yudain accepted immediately.

An editor, not an entrepreneur, Yudain didn't enjoy the sale process. He had been receiving legal advice from an old friend in Connecticut who specialized in divorce law. He later retained a Washington, D. C., corporate attorney. His sister, who handled the paper's accounting and advertising, prepared a statement of financial condition and five-year profit and loss. He recalls, "The sale was semi-painful because it's so alien to me. It was fascinating in a way, but it also took a lot of time and I was still putting out the paper. Especially the figures—I hated that. I had to go through circulation, subscriptions, how many paid, how many owed, who owed. It was very time-consuming and very boring."

From the first lunch to closing day, the sale of *Roll Call* took three months. Yudain vividly remembers flying to New York on a windy, rainy Thursday, catching a bus from the airport and walking to the Park Avenue offices of the buyer's attorneys. He arrived at the building, windblown and disheveled, as Levitt's limousine pulled up. Waiting for Yudain in the law offices was a message from his Connecticut lawyer: "Do not sign anything until you call me." His old friend had discovered something in the sales agreement that would have cost Yudain a $50,000 tax bill. "That caused quite a stir," Yudain recounts. "They wanted to know why we waited until the last moment to make this change. There was a little squabble, but they worked it out."

He continues, "Levitt handed me a check—wrote it out and tossed it over like a beanbag." The sale completed, everyone headed in separate directions. Levitt lent Yudain his limousine for the afternoon so he didn't have to scramble for the bus.

# CHAPTER 5

# FINDING A BUYER

"Being approached is one thing. Going out and trying to sell a company is another. I don't know how to find a buyer. I would consider merging with a competitor or with someone selling complementary product lines."

—Shannon Edwards

## ONE SELLER'S STORY: Holly Manor Nursing Home

Ken Rothman was confident as he began his search for a buyer for Holly Manor Nursing Home in New Jersey. The health care industry was booming and his 114-bed facility was an attractive property. His optimism was reinforced by regular letters from buyers eager to talk to any nursing home seller. He had ignored the letters for years, but knew they represented his ticket out.

Rothman owned and managed Holly Manor for thirteen years. His parents built it and he took over after college. Running a nursing home is not a nine-to-five office job. Rothman explains: "Everything, literally everything, would eventually find its way to me. If there's ants in the room, if the roof is falling in, if the payroll needs signing. When I went home my phone would ring several times in the evening. When I'd go on vacation I'd leave a number and get three calls a day. You really don't get out of it."

Tired and burned out, Rothman hoped to find a buyer quickly. He says, "I had these letters and I consulted the trade magazines —they always have advertising for businesses. The 'I-want-to-buy' ads. I had twenty-five different places to go looking, and I started to make my piles. I knew what kind of purchaser I wanted. I weeded out the individual buyer, thinking he would be unreliable. The only assets he would have would be the facility, which would mean a large mortgage and little cash up front." Rothman's reasoning is understandable, but not all individual buyers are cash-poor or need a highly leveraged acquisition. Some active individual buyers are very wealthy people.

Rothman continues, "I looked at the other end and said 'no' to large chain corporations that have hundreds of nursing homes. They don't care about an individual facility that much, and I still cared about my facility. I decided the buyer would be a small chain—somebody who had ten homes, twelve homes, something like that. Not large but growing."

With a firm idea of the kind of buyer he was seeking, Rothman took the direct route and gambled on a cold call. "Taking the twenty-five places, I narrowed it down to two names. I knew them only by reputation—what I read in trade magazines. I called the first phone number and asked to speak to the vice president in charge. Five minutes later I was talking with him."

The two men swapped facts about their companies—age of facilities, size, kinds of revenues. The vice president of Columbia Corporation, an aggressive acquirer that had bought more than thirty homes, asked the essential question in nursing home economics: What was the patient mix? The percentage of patients paying under Medicare, Medicaid or private plans determines the value of a home. Holly Manor had a fifty-fifty mix (public to private patients), gross income just under $3 million and after-tax net income just under $150,000. After talking for thirty minutes, they promised to Express Mail each other financials and management details.

For a public buyer, sharing financials is a simple matter of sending published statements. A private company's financials, however, may be confidential and give away competitive information.

A seller should withhold figures until the buyer has signed a confidentiality agreement.

Rothman received enough material the next day to establish that the buyer was sincere and capable. The telling documents were inspection reports from state health departments. "By knowing the result of these inspections at a facility, it is easy to trickle back and find out how management works," Rothman explains. "In each state the department of health goes to a facility at least once a year, unannounced, and does a survey. If you find out, for example, that they have absolutely rotten housekeeping, you get an idea that they're not interested in spending money for staff or supplies. These documents are probably the easiest way to find out the philosophy of a company."

Knowing his industry and where to look for information, Rothman took one additional step to check out his buyer. He telephoned a state health department where one of their facilities was located. He recalls, "I asked for the survey. By the time I got to someone who knew anything, I just said, 'What's the story? Are these people any good?' And they said, 'Yeah, we don't have any problem with them.' " That was good enough for Rothman.

The men talked by phone Tuesday, Wednesday and Thursday, each checking off a list of questions and negotiation items. They broached the subject of price in rough terms: the vice president introduced a range of $3 million to $4 million. Rothman reports, "After I said, 'Yes, I'm willing to sell in this bracket,' he was happy with the highest figure, and I knew I would be willing to accept the bottom figure."

Friday's mail brought Rothman an exceptionally brief letter of intent from Columbia Corporation. It contained little legal boilerplate and a price within a broad 25 percent range to be determined by negotiation. One page, two paragraphs and a description of the companies and the buyer's intention to purchase Holly Manor assets for between $3 million and $4 million. Rothman signed it immediately.

They still had lots of ground to cover. Rothman informed his attorney and accountant of the pending sale. He kept their roles strictly within their areas of expertise and did not consult them on his decision or the letter of intent. Since the buyer wanted to purchase assets, both advised Rothman to liquidate his company under Internal Revenue Code Section 337 and distribute the assets within twelve months and so avoid taxes on his gains. (The 1986 Tax Reform Act eliminated this option for most sellers. However, for sales under $5 million, this option is available through 1988.)

Rothman had an idea of what his business was worth long before he found a buyer. Three years earlier, when his father was selling his stock to Rothman, they hired an independent appraiser. "I found out that nursing homes sell according to a per bed figure," Rothman relates. "Like a hospital or hotel. Not by the square footage, but by the number of revenue-producing units. In New Jersey at that time, nursing homes beds were going for $28,000 to $38,000 per bed. The higher figure would be for those that have the high private patient mix."

Rothman was ready for negotiations, a rapid-fire exchange of numbers. The buyer jumped in first with an offer. Rothman felt it was low and named his figure. They settled on $33,000 per bed for a total price of $3.8 million. The buyer gave Rothman the liberty to define the terms—any combination from all cash to 90 percent notes. Rothman asked for 70 percent cash and the balance in a ten-year, 10 percent note.

Columbia Corporation was a knowledgeable, experienced buyer. For Rothman, this meant streamlined negotiations and efficient due diligence. The buyer inspected Holly Manor in less than an hour. "The guy said, 'I've been doing this so long that I know what I'm looking for and looking at,' " Rothman remembers. "He'd see a bed and could instantly identify it, figure out its age, and know everything about it." They reviewed the purchase agreement—a dense twenty-five pages—with the same dispatch.

But no sale is trouble-free, especially if a government agency is involved. While Rothman and Columbia glided through negotiations and paperwork, the state of New Jersey was bringing the transaction to a dead stop.

After Rothman signed the asset purchase agreement in mid-February, the buyer applied to the state health planning agency for a certificate allowing the facility to change ownership. A sale was legally impossible until they received the certificate. Months passed. Rothman grew impatient: he wanted out and he wanted his money. In May he told the buyer that if they drew up the papers and paid a monthly fee, he would sign over the management of Holly Manor. Columbia assumed control in June. But still no certificate. June passed. Unwilling to wait any longer, Rothman directed the buyer to draw up two sets of closing documents, one completing the transaction with the certificate and another for depositing the money into an escrow account should they not receive the certificate. Closing day was scheduled for July 31 regardless of whether they had the document. The day before, the buyer's attorney personally picked up the certificate from the state health agency. The next afternoon, Holly Manor Nursing Home had a new owner.

## PUT YOUR COMPANY IN PLAY

Buyers are everywhere. They're the fellow sitting next to you on the plane, the person at the end of the dais at a business luncheon, a face in an annual report, an executive quoted in a trade publication or *Forbes*. They're public and private companies, individuals and groups of investors. They're active lookers or listeners who unintentionally become acquirers.

When a company is in play a seller has fully prepped it. He or she has assessed its strengths and weaknesses and identified potential buyers and obstacles. The company is ready to make its debut. Buyers begin to notice it. Some may have quietly inquired about its accomplishments. Although bidding wars for well-known companies unfold in the newspaper every morning, most exchanges are quiet and private. Putting a company in play doesn't require running an advertisement or issuing a press release. Just the opposite. It's discreetly letting buyers know you're prepared and willing. It's avoiding the look of an anxious seller whose company, like a sale table on December 26, has been picked over by every passerby. (We talk later about the shopworn look.) Sellers find and approach buyers behind-the-scenes and with a lowered voice.

Buyers are at any business gathering—trade shows, business seminars, public meetings, professional associations, fund-raisers, charity events—even your own company functions when guests include suppliers and clients. A remarkable number of buyers and sellers connect through casual contact, mutal acquaintances, chance meetings and plain coincidences. In a routine week an owner encounters numerous candidates—suppliers, clients, brokers, competitors, friends, neighbors. Regardless of how methodically you search for a buyer, odds are even that you already know him or her and you'll meet as buyer-seller by chance.

All right, so here you are at the monthly Rotary luncheon, now what? You strike up conversations. Talk to people. Introduce yourself and your company, ask what they do, and find a common interest. Drop a few impressive facts about your company. Don't brag, just let the listener know your business is healthy and profitable and growing. No need to declare your wish to sell. Buyers prick up their ears at the sound of any attractive company. At any business function exchange business cards. If you feel awkward quip that you admire the Japanese and keep handing out cards.

Perhaps the best way to find buyers is to become one yourself. Sure, you've resolved to sell your company, and you will. But as a strategy for locating buyers, talk with other sellers and watch the mergers and acquisitions marketplace. This isn't a suggestion to assume a false pretense. You probably would buy a company given the right financing, structure and circumstances. It may be unlikely but not impossible.

Assume temporarily that you are a bona fide buyer. Follow acquistion activity in publications such as *Mergers & Acquisitions* and *Journal of Buyouts and Acquisitions*. Subscribing to these will put you on mailing lists to receive notices about seminars, conferences and forthcoming books. One person's junk mail is another's required reading, and some of these circulars announce worthwhile events and resources, and opportunities to meet buyers. Don't advertise in these, just watch what other buyers and sellers are doing. Notice how other companies are locating and contacting buyers.

## INVESTMENT BANKERS AND BUSINESS BROKERS TRACK BUYERS

Investment bankers and business brokers know from personal contacts, the business press and buyers themselves what companies are in an "acquisition mode." (They talk that way.) It is no secret which companies are buying—their names appear regularly in the business press and trade publications. Buyers are secretive about *whom* they're talking to, but not about being an active purchaser.

Just as important as company names are the individuals responsible for acquisitions. Some companies have entire departments devoted to acquisitions or "new business development." In others, a single individual is responsible for scouting prospects. Investment bankers, business brokers, acquisition consultants and lawyers know these people. While anyone can read that such firms as General Electric and American Express Company are prowling for properties, acquisition specialists know what they are looking for and who is leading the search.

A seller, consulting with an investment banker or business broker, compiles a list of prime candidates. A seller's board of directors may know of prospects. These are the most likely buyers. Usually no more than five companies or individuals have profiles and acquisition goals that fit the seller's. The list is expanded only when these prospects decline.

Exactly which firm a seller and scouts approach first depends on how well they know their target and a seller's objectives. What kind of buyer does the seller want? Someone to pay top dollar? Someone who will treat employees right?

If money is the main goal the investment banker or broker may auction the company to a number of buyers. A seller with other goals avoids an auction and hunts for another type of buyer. This buyer may give the seller a role in the company or allow it to operate as an independent subsidiary. Perhaps the ideal buyer will infuse new capital.

Business brokers and investment bankers are useful in screening buyers and learning who is financially qualified and able to complete an acquisition. They know the companies or individuals who look but never buy, who bid for a company but don't have the money or access to financing, or whose management style and plans are unacceptable to a seller.

There is no formula or pattern for how business brokers and investment bankers operate. Their value is connections, experience and identifying buyers.

## WATCH FOR WINDOW-SHOPPERS

> "We had a good rapport. We laid everything on the table. That was the one thing I liked about their business: they are a business of their word. They had a track record of doing what they said they would do. I felt it was important to turn this little business of mine to someone who had the same ethics as I did."
> —Dee Weitzel

A seller should closely inspect any buyer who survives the initial screening. "Initial screening" entails a meeting to see if people are ready to talk. This first meeting usually accomplishes little of substance: buyer and seller explore the chemistry between them (personality clashes or unrealistic expectations can kill a deal at the starting line) and decide whether and how to proceed.

Window-shoppers—lookers with no serious intention of making a purchase—are hard to spot. Because they are frequently experienced shoppers, they know the acquisitions marketplace and the language. Their purpose is not to buy, however, but to compare prices with their own business, scout the competition or simply fantasize. Some people are only interested in buying a $2 bill for $1. A shopper looking only for information may request financial, market and operating reports from a seller. However, serious requests do not make a serious buyer.

Weed out shoppers by turning the tables: ask a buyer to produce corporate financial statements, tax returns and operating details. Financials separate the dilettante from the dedicated. Look for sufficient earnings and assets, free of heavy debt, to finance or at least leverage an acquisition. A sincere buyer has enough for a deposit and the resources to obtain financing either from a third party or the seller, or to pay with stock. Also ask a would-be buyer about its acquisition history. Has it purchased other companies?

Get names and dates. Though someone has to be first, proceed with caution if it's you.

Sellers don't have to depend on buyers for information. Market, financial and legal information is available elsewhere. Here is where to find it:

**SECURITIES AND EXCHANGE COMMISSION:** Public companies must file the following financial information with the SEC, and these reports are available to the public. (The SEC is relatively flexible about requirements for very small public companies and may not have all this information on them.) (450 5th Street, N.W., Washington, DC 20549)

- Annual financial report and statement of financial condition (Report 10-K)
- Quarterly financial report (Report 10-Q)
- Significant changes in financial condition such as an asset purchase, bankruptcy or resignation of a director (Report 8-Q)
- Annual report of employee stock purchase plan (Report 11-K)
- List of shareholders acquiring 5 percent or more of company stock (Report 13-D)

**STANDARD AND POOR'S CORPORATION:** "Corporation Records" on more than 12,000 companies, on-line data on 6,500 companies, stock market reports, and handbooks on industries and trading markets. (25 Broadway, New York, NY 10004)

**MOODY'S INVESTORS SERVICE:** "Corporation Reports" and "Credit Reports" on 20,000 public companies, and reports on 5,000 foreign companies. (99 Church Street, New York, NY 10007)

**DUN & BRADSTREET CORPORATION:** "Business Information Reports" on corporations, covering financial condition, management and operating history are available to subscribers. Dun & Bradstreet has 7 million companies in its data base and will prepare a report on any company. (299 Park Avenue, New York, NY 10171)

**TRW BUSINESS CREDIT SERVICES:** "Business Profiles" on individual companies, covering banking information, key facts, management, finances, payment and credit experience, and public record information are available to subscribers. (505 City Parkway West, Orange, CA 92668)

**W. T. GRIMM & COMPANY:** This company collects industry data on mergers and acquisitions and publishes them in the annual *Mergerstat Review*. It also offers consulting services to buyers and sellers. (135 South La Salle Street, Chicago, IL 60603)

Information on private companies is harder to come by. It's the nature of private companies to avoid releasing details about their businesses. Researching a private company requires poking around a number of places—asking questions people may not answer—and assembling information piecemeal. Dun & Bradstreet and TRW Business Credit Services report on private companies, although the financials may be sketchy.

Industry trade associations are a source, and *Gale's Encyclopedia of Associations* lists most of them. Trade associations have information on members, although it may be general. Industry associations also publish reference books listing companies, both public and private, and credit histories. For instance, there is the *Produce Blue Book* and the *Lumbermen's Red Book* for these industries. Credit reporting agencies may know if a company is in financial trouble.

Banks are useful, and the most effective way to extract information is from bank to bank. Ask your bank to inquire at a buyer's bank for a "trade check." Some banks are as informative as a Dun & Bradstreet report. The credit inquiry office may provide details about a company's average balance, financial health, number of years in business and general credit history.

## CASTING ABROAD

Foreigners buy hundreds of U.S. companies, and not only mega-corps. While foreigners have acquired such companies as the Chicago *Sun Times*, Grand Union supermarkets, Carnation, and Peoples Drug Stores, they have also picked up an assortment of small, privately owned companies—sugar beet factories, newsletter publishers, trucking equipment companies, electrical manufacturers. The CEO of an English waste-management firm voices a preference shared by other overseas buyers: "Many of the 10,000 companies in the field are small, family-owned concerns which are very attractive acquisition candidates for a large, well-capitalized firm like ours."

The most active foreign buyers come from Japan, the United Kingdom, Hong Kong, Canada, France, Sweden, the Netherlands and West Germany. Foreigners like buying American. The decline in the value of the dollar relative to other currencies, low interest rates and ready access to financing make American companies more affordable. The stable U.S. political system suits offshore owners —no coups d'etat or nationalization. And buying American offers a shortcut for foreigners lagging in research and development in semiconductors, electronics, manufacturing processes, biotechnology, chemicals and communications. Lastly, foreigners have discovered that buying here offers a foothold in growing consumer markets.

Foreign buyers look for companies in sectors where they have experience, such as manufacturing, retailing, service businesses and agriculture. They favor mundane, basic industries or new technology that fills gaps or enhances their domestic operations. It's rare for a foreigner to branch into a new industry through an American acquisition.

Some American firms are seemingly beyond foreigners' grasp because the U.S. government limits or prohibits non-U.S. ownership of certain domestic industries. (Although one buyer changed his citizenship to get around this prohibition.) These industries cover coastal shipping, towing and salvage, vessel documentation and transfer, air transportation, radio and television, communications satellites, mineral resources, nuclear energy, geothermal energy and government defense contractors.

Foreigners' eagerness to enter the American market inclines them to pay premium prices. They frequently outbid American buyers and offer more than book value or higher earnings multiples. From their point of view, buying American makes sense. Compared with businesses in other countries and given the value of the dollar, American firms look almost cheap. Another foreign charm is they often pay all cash because they cannot use their stock in the United States. Once ensconced in an American company, foreign owners are generally more patient and don't demand instant returns on their investments.

Typically, foreign owners keep American managers, especially if the acquisition represents an unfamiliar market. Occasionally, a knowledgeable foreigner wants to share operating control. A seller should get a sense of a foreigner's plans before closing. Otherwise, mismatched expectations can hurt a sale. A complete hands-off relationship is rare with a foreign owner. An American manager should be ready to travel regularly to foreign headquarters and have a foreign watchdog. Regardless of how amicable the sale or how well buyer and seller fit, cultural clashes are inevitable. Not only do languages and management styles vary, but so also do attitudes toward timetables, salaries, benefits, promotions and operating philosophies.

Finding a foreign buyer is a little more complicated than booking a European vacation, but not much. The best approach is through an intermediary—an investment banking firm or business broker that knows foreign buyers, or the U.S. representative of a foreign company. Many Japanese, English and West German companies have American offices, and locating them can be as simple as thumbing a New York telephone book. Intermediaries should be used for introductions and names of individuals responsible for American acquisitions in the native country.

International trade fairs and foreign conferences are a fertile ground for picking up names of active foreign buyers. If you've identified a foreign buyer but it doesn't have a U.S. representative, and investment bankers do not know the firm, go straight to the source. Overseas telephones work fine and English is spoken worldwide.

## LEVERAGED BUYOUTS

Mention **leverage buyout** and people think of mountains of debt and managers banding together to buy out their boss. Or executives taking a company private to protect it from raiders. Leveraged buyouts frequently involve managers purchasing a company from its owner. These informed buyers are intimately familiar with their target. They know operations, finances, management and future prospects firsthand. In short, they're not strangers buying an operation they learned about months earlier. If the traditional buyer-seller deal is akin to the courtship and marriage of a fresh-faced bride, a leveraged buyout by insiders is like tying the knot with a relative.

Some leveraged buyouts resemble a more conventional romance. These are instigated not by company management but by outsiders. In an outside LBO the buyer is a consortium of a financial packager and a management group. The first may be an investment banking firm, professional investor, investment group, small business investment company or a venture capital company; the second is an individual, former owner, a management group recruited by the financial people, or a company. All these players complicate an LBO—negotiations alone may involve five or six interested parties, plus lawyers and accountants. To cut through this crowd, sellers first seek out financial backers.

The financial packagers orchestrate a leveraged buyout. They decide which company to buy, negotiate terms and payment schedules, and arrange financing. Because a leveraged buyout imposes a large debt on a selling company, which it pays out of operating cash or by liquidating assets, buyout financers are very choosy about their companies.

The brass ring for LBO buyers is cash. They want a company generating cash through revenues and earnings or by selling off assets. They've found that companies with these features are the best cash cows:

- A low-tech ("mature") business such as a manufacturer or distributor. This kind of company usually doesn't require additional capital and has the cash flow to pay its debt. Its products or services have a proven market. A high-tech business may need substantial investment, and its cash flow can be cyclical or undependable. Service companies that depend on people who frequently change jobs are also not good LBO candidates.
- Substantial fixed, tangible or liquid assets that can be used either as loan collateral or sold off to reduce debt. These assets have to be substantially larger than the debt against them. They also have to be in good working condition. Assets on the edge of obsolescence or needing replacement require money the LBO buyer does not want to pay.
- Slow, steady earnings over the past five years. Leveraged buyers want a company with a dependable, constant earnings stream. An important feature of earnings is a record of constant cash flow so the LBO buyer can confidently expect this flow to continue.
- Little or no debt. Debt with its insistent interest payments reduces available cash. Long-term liabilities and considerable accounts payable effectively reduce the amount of available cash.
- Management able to work under the new financial structure and cope with the pressure of heavy debt. These managers may be in the company or recruited from outside by the financial people.

Here's a simplified version of how an outside LBO operates. A company for sale approaches an investment banking firm. The sellers and key managers are eager to sell but stay on and are prepared to saddle the company with substantial debt. The purchase price of the company is funded by lenders, third-party investors and, in small part, managers. The company pays back the principal, plus a rewarding return on their investment, by selling off assets or from cash flow.

Investment bankers negotiate price based on an assessment of the breakup value of assets and future cash flow. Aiming to eliminate debt within five years, they start bidding at a multiple of pretax cash flow (this multiple in recent years has been around five). Of course, companies with valuable liquid assets, unrealized tax benefits, strong earnings streams or other hidden assets sell for more.

Leveraged buyers hope to pay off the debt within a fixed timetable. The timetable depends on the industry. A steel company may pay off in less than five years while a cable company can take fifteen years. Buyers also aim for a 30 percent or more annual rate of return on equity.

Terms of a sale price—the kinds of debt—concern the buyer more than a seller who walks away with all cash while the leveraged buyer acquires a raft of partners and creditors. If the seller has to hold a note, it is a different story. Leveraged buyers assume three levels (called tiers) of debt. They pledge liquid assets, such as accounts receivable and working capital, for secured financing (about 60–70 percent of the purchase price) and subordinated loans (about 15–20 percent and called **mezzanine financing**). About 15–20 percent of the purchase price comes from selling common and/ or preferred stock to managers and outside investors.

If an LBO proceeds according to plan, the new owners get their money back and a handsome return. Then they either sell the company, go public or do another LBO. If a company cannot pay off the debt an owner may see his equity disappear and the business chopped to pieces or plunged into bankruptcy. An LBO is not for the fainthearted.

Though LBOs are associated with large companies—Safeway Stores, Beatrice and Macy's were leveraged into the laps of new owners—small companies can participate too. Financial experts reckon that a company with annual sales of more than $1 million and after-tax earnings of more than $75,000 may qualify. Another consideration is transaction costs. An LBO runs up substantial fees for attorneys, accountants and investment bankers. A seller has to weigh whether the size of an LBO justifies the fees required to accomplish it.

Sellers who have managers willing to buy may prefer an LBO. With an LBO a company can keep its shape and employees, provided it pays its notes on time. Sellers may opt to stay with their leveraged company and find they are more comfortable than with a new corporate owner.

## AVOID THE SHOPWORN LOOK

A company on the market month after month, year after year, looks shopworn. Paraded past a host of buyers and a permanent fixture on brokers' listings, a company loses its appeal, to say nothing of the effect on productivity and employee morale. The lack of movement and shopworn look may have little to do with the company's desirability. Even a distressed business can find a buyer if the seller goes about it right. The shopworn look comes from *how* a company is put on the market, not from the company itself. A seller who has an unrealistic idea of a company's worth or is trying to sell when similar companies are not moving will meet resistance or indifference.

Sellers make a mistake advertising. Publicly announcing a sale in the business press or trade publications says two things about a company. First, it implies a seller has not found a buyer through private channels, suggesting something is wrong. Second, an advertisement destroys the possibility of a confidential transaction. Employees, clients and suppliers can see immediately that the company is advertising for sale. Knowing a company is for sale can damage employee morale and business contacts. And buyers don't like blind ads. Blind ads are either too secretive or coy.

If there's little interest or many shoppers but no takers, a seller should take a company off the market to avoid looking picked over. Instead of grabbing at last resorts and advertising, a seller should cease sale activity for six months. Notify business brokers and investment bankers and other intermediaries that the company is no longer for sale. This time can be used to examine the sale offering, figure out why it wasn't selling and spruce it up.

## WATCH FOR ROADBLOCKS

Antitrust laws are a bigger worry for a buyer than a seller, but his worries are yours when you're trying to consummate a sale. Questions of competition, market share, monopolistic behavior and restraint of trade arise when buyers are considering an acquisition as well as afterward. By and large, buyers are responsible for ensuring a deal does not violate federal laws or regulations. Although the Department of Justice or Federal Trade Commission makes the final decision on the legality of a proposed acquisition, the buyer's lawyers should know if they must apply for a ruling.

Unless you merge with your main competitor to achieve a dominant market position, antitrust laws generally do not affect sellers of small companies. But that is a generalization. If you think one of these issues may apply to your sale, run it by an attorney.

Antitrust restrictions may ruin a sale or delay it to the point of extinction. Sellers are not completely free of responsibility. One provision of an antitrust law—the Hart-Scott-Rodino Act—is aimed specifically at them. Here's a summary of antitrust laws and guidelines that might apply to your sale:

> *Federal Trade Commission Act:*   Prohibits unfair competition that might create a monopoly, and false or deceptive advertising.
>
> *Sherman Act:*   Prohibits companies from joining together if the combination would restrain trade or monopolize a business. Makes illegal price-fixing, boycotts and competitors agreeing to split territories.
>
> *Clayton Act, Section 7:*   Prohibits company acquisitions that *may* lessen competition or tend to create a monopoly. Applies if an acquisition raises the possibility of reduced competition or a monopoly.
>
> *Hart-Scott-Rodino Act:*   Requires certain buyers and sellers to notify the Federal Trade Commission and Department of Justice of a pending acquisition and wait for approval. Rules are complex, but generally either of the following conditions rates a red flag: (1) One party has sales or assets of $100 million or more and the other has

sales or assets of $10 million or more; and (2) If the sale gives the buyer 15 percent or more of the selling company or more than $15 million in value of the stock or assets of the seller.

*Herfindahl-Hirschman Index:*   Department of Justice guidelines imposing a mathematical formula measuring potential market concentration. If the combined market concentration of two companies exceeds a certain level the government will oppose a sale. Because the guidelines are applied to all companies within a market, even the smallest acquisition may be affected. The government uses a formula but is not totally rigid. It examines potential acquisitions on a case-by-case basis, taking into account how easily other companies can enter a market, foreign competition, a changing market, and whether one of the companies involved is in financial trouble.

## LETTER OF INTENT: FISH OR CUT BAIT

> "They put money into escrow when we laid out the client list on the table and signed the letter of intent. Kind of a good-faith payment."
> —Dee Weitzel

A letter of intent (also called **memo of intent, memo of understanding, agreement in principle**) separates the dreamers and lookers from the movers and shakers. This is the first formal step in an acquisition, although it's usually not legally binding because it contains substantial conditions such as being subject to approval by boards of directors. (Legally, some letters of intent can be read either way so lawyers always have to be involved in their drafting. The $3 billion Texaco payment to Pennzoil without a written contract should make every seller cautious.) It's usually conditional on due diligence. It spells out a buyer's intention to purchase a company and conditions of a sale. It usually imposes a timetable and specifies a purchase price. The price may be expressed as a formula or criteria for calculating it, an exact number or a range. Other areas of agreement may be mentioned, such as whether stock or assets will be sold or who pays finder's or business broker's fees. The letter may be a couple of paragraphs or a few pages, but rarely longer.

The buyer prepares a letter of intent. (A seller represented by an investment banker may write the letter, although it's unusual.) Before signing, a seller should feel completely comfortable with the deal, know exactly how to move to closing and consult an attorney. An important consequence of signing is that the buyer usually requires the seller to cease looking for a buyer. Until the sale is consummated or negotiations are terminated, the selling company is off the market.

A letter of intent is miles from a done deal. It's just the proposal, and much can happen during engagement, but it advances the sale process from flirting to formal engagement.

An anxious buyer wanting a more binding arrangement than a letter of intent may offer a purchase option. By giving the seller a nonrefundable deposit that may or may not be applied to the purchase price, the buyer ensures that a seller doesn't talk to other buyers. An option guarantees that a buyer can purchase a company regardless of other offers. Writing an option is more legally complicated than a letter of intent. If a purchase option is signed buyer and seller have probably agreed on many of the terms of the final agreement.

What does a seller get from an option besides money? Reassurance that the buyer wants the company. But the downside is a pair of silver handcuffs. A seller cannot talk to other buyers and shop the company. The sale is locked in until the option expires or the buyer decides not to exercise it.

What follows is an example of a letter of intent between a large, publicly held buyer and a smaller seller.

[SAMPLE LETTER OF INTENT]
(Buyer's letterhead stationery)

Seller
Company Name
Street address
City, State

Re: Acquisition of Seller and Company

Dear Jim:

This letter will confirm the understanding reached between Buyer, Inc., a Delaware corporation, and Seller and Company, a California corporation, concerning the possible combination of our two companies.

1. *Purchase.* It is contemplated that Buyer and Seller will enter into a Definitive Agreement providing for the acquisition of all the outstanding shares of Seller and Company.

2. *Purchase Price.* The outstanding Seller and Company common stock shall be purchased for the following consideration:

   (a) An aggregate of 162,890 shares of Buyer, Inc., common stock;

   (b) Five Million Three Hundred Twenty Thousand and No/ 100 Dollars ( $5,320,000) in immediately available funds;

3. *Conditions to be contained in the Definitive Agreement.* The following conditions shall be contained in the Definitive Agreement and will be conditions precedent to the purchase and sale:

   (a) Delivery of favorable legal opinions by counsel.

   (b) At the closing date, the financial condition of Seller and Company will be as shown in the July 31, 198_ balance sheet, except as modified by changes occurring thereafter in the normal course of business. Purchase price changed upward if net worth on closing exceeds _____ or reduced or canceled if below _____.

   (c) Receipt of assurances satisfactory to Buyer of the continuity of the present management of Seller and Company.

(d) Between the date hereof and the closing date, there shall have been no material adverse change in the business, operations, assets or properties of Seller and Company.

4. *The Definitive Agreement.* The Definitive Agreement shall contain standard covenants, conditions and warranties, including warranties relating to the financial condition and business of Buyer, Inc. The purchase and sale will be subject to the approval of the Boards of Directors and shareholders of Buyer and Seller and Company. The Definitive Agreement will also provide for a mutually satisfactory escrow arrangement to protect Buyer from any contingent liabilities and litigation pending or prior to closing.

5. *Information and Access.* Buyer will conduct its normal acquisition study including making a detailed review of prior operating results and current financial condition. Seller and Company will give Buyer and its representatives access during normal business hours to all properties, books, contracts, documents and records with respect to its affairs. Buyer will maintain the confidentiality of any information it receives in accordance with its confidentiality agreement with Seller and Company.

6. *No Other Negotiations.* During the period from the date of this letter until December 31, 198_, Seller and Company will not enter into discussions or negotiations with any other party regarding the transactions contemplated herein; *provided, however,* nothing shall prohibit Seller and Company from discharging any obligation it may have to advise its shareholders of the existence of any unsolicited proposal from a third party.

7. *Closing Date.* The Definitive Agreement will set forth a specific date as to which the transaction will close. We will each use our best efforts to make sure that Closing is on or before December 31, 198_.

8. *Expenses.* The parties acknowledge that no broker or finder is entitled to any brokerage or finder's fees or other commission in connection with the proposed acquisition. The shareholders of each company will bear their respective costs and expenses with

respect to negotiation, preparation and execution of the Definitive Agreement.

9. *Nondisclosure*. We will each use our best efforts to keep this Letter of Intent confidential and will reveal it only to directors, auditors, key officers and employees, attorneys, consultants and shareholders.

10. *Absence of Enforceable Agreement*. Except for the terms and provisions of this section and of Sections 5, 6, 8 and 9, this document is not an enforceable agreement between us but merely a general statement of intent that sets forth the general basis for the preparation of the Definitive Agreement.

If this letter agrees with your understanding, please sign the enclosed copy and return it to us on or before October 15, 198_, after which date this letter will otherwise not be in effect.

Sincerely,

Chairman, Buyer, Inc.

Accepted this ____ day of November 198_.

Chairman, Seller and Company

---

## ONE SELLER'S STORY: New England Inn

The pool of potential buyers for some businesses is deep. Buying a country inn appeals to many people—escapees from city life and high-rise jobs, rural entrepreneurs, companies that manage resort properties, hotel companies, real estate developers and even investment groups. When Joe and Linda Johnston decided to sell their thirty-nine-room inn they knew finding a buyer would be the easy part. One possible purchaser had broached the subject two years before they even dreamed of cashing in.

Nevertheless, instead of relying on fortuitous encounters, the Johnstons retained a business broker specializing in the New En-

gland hostelry market. For $10,000 he signed a one-year agreement
to contact buyers if the first prospect fell through. The Johnstons
also asked the business broker to help them avoid paying a real
estate commission to any buyer. They had discovered that some
buyers in New Hampshire held real estate licenses and demanded
a 6 percent commission when they purchased a business composed
mostly of property.

When the Johnstons bought the New England Inn, a converted
farmhouse built in 1809, it needed extensive repairs. They invested
$500,000 to refurbish rooms, modernize plumbing and wiring, and
improve the kitchen. But like most old houses, the inn needed
constant repairs, and the Johnstons faced another $500,000 in-
vestment. They had owned the business for seven years and were
burned-out. "We were tired of working and being broke all the
time. We were looking at a payback that would take another five
to eight years, and we weren't ready to commit to that kind of time.
We had gotten to the point psychologically that it would be good
for us to sell out and let someone else take care of it," says Joe
Johnston.

Business brokers cultivate buyers and sellers, establishing a
network of businesses although the businesses may not change hands
for years. The Johnstons' business broker had stayed in touch with
them since they first moved in. Acting as a general consultant, he
periodically offered advice on the inn's financial statements. At
selling time the business broker's role grew. "He represented us to
the buyer by putting all our numbers together," Joe Johnston
explains. "He had the final say as far as the price was concerned
—justifying it, making the initial contact, ironing out details. When
we signed a letter of intent he phased out and we did the final
negotiating."

The business broker contacted the first interested buyer, Baron
Resources Corporation, an investment company that sold limited
partnerships in country inns. As general partner, Baron Resources
found investors and managed properties. Because the firm owned
other inns, the Johnstons knew owners who had sold to them and
were pleased with the outcome.

At the first meeting the Johnstons, their business broker and
the buyer debated the price. To value the inn, the Johnstons ex-

amined revenues—$700,000 to $800,000 a year—and 10 percent earnings. They figured it was worth around two and a half times gross. On the other side of the table, the buyer estimated the value at eight and a half times net earnings. "Everybody had their own separate formula," Joe says. The Johnstons' starting price was $1.9 million, which included $300,000 for Joe to manage a nearby townhouse development that he had an interest in, but which was unrelated to the inn property.

Negotiations moved swiftly with buyer and seller agreeing on a price within twenty-four hours of meeting each other. "When we were ready to sell they were ready to buy," Joe relates. "It didn't take much time. We knew the least amount we would take—$1.5 million—and they agreed to that. At the same time we made a separate agreement for the townhouse management."

This was not a textbook sale, however. Finding a buyer and coming to terms were simple compared with structuring the financing. As an investment group, the buyer sold partnership units to raise the money to purchase inns. Until the 1986 Tax Reform Act, it had successfully funded numerous acquisitions by offering tax deductions. But the new law dampened investor interest in tax shelters, and the buyer couldn't attract sufficient investors. The Johnstons accepted a $5,000 deposit on signing the letter of intent, then waited while the buyer rewrote its marketing plan and shifted emphasis from saving taxes to return on investment.

The Johnstons could not have anticipated financing difficulties. Other inn sellers had no trouble with sales funded by partnership units. In hindsight, Joe would not have allowed his business to be off the market and the sale to hang for such a small deposit. He would have demanded more, and if the buyer did not have cash he would have pushed for a mortgage and note.

The two parties went back and forth on the mix of cash and notes. They were not far apart. Because the buyer did not have the entire purchase price in cash, the Johnstons accepted partial payment in a mortgage and reduced their taxes. As a negotiator, Joe was tough yet accommodating. "In selling an inn of our size, you can get very emotional," he explains. "Leave emotions outside the door. Deal very, very businesslike. Know what your price is and that it's a marketable price. And once you have a buyer, be as cooperative as possible. There's nothing worse than having a buyer and seller mad at one another."

The sale of the New England Inn to the first buyer closed four months after everyone shook hands on the price. The buyer paid $200,000 in the form of eight limited partnership units (essentially these were notes bearing 9 percent interest), $300,000 in a twenty-year second mortgage paying between 8 and 11 percent, and $1 million cash.

Looking back, Joe Johnston discovered that the inn sale created an unexpected dilemma. Fifty-four years old, he is too young to retire and eager for more challenges. He reflects, "We went through a ten-hour sale and it was a little hairy at times. But the toughest part of the decision is, What next?"

| CHAPTER | THE NEGOTIATION |
| :---: | :---: |
| **6** | **DANCE** |

"The general tenor was that both sides wanted to do the deal. If we could do it and they could do it without negatively affecting earnings per share, they wanted it. No one was bluffing."  —Bill King

Negotiations are like the decathlon—a series of challenges where perseverance and tactics count as much as skill. You enter every event and you win some and lose some. In the end, the total score—the shape and substance of a sale—is more important than the individual parts.

Negotiations follow no set routine. In one sale they may consist of two or three friendly meetings at the seller's office and lead to an immediate agreement. In another they laboriously stretch over months and hop among hotel rooms across the country. It all depends on the complexity of the transaction and the attitudes and styles of the participants.

There are no rights or wrongs, no acceptable or unacceptable ways to proceed. Even professionals who have sat through dozens of deals say no two go the same way. Sure, people use similar techniques and some bargainers are better than others. But it is the character of each sale and of the personalities that define how negotiations unfold and the final outcome.

A little spadework helps before talking. A seller should cull and think through the most important points ahead of time and create a scenario or series of positions on each. A seller has a dozen or more issues that have to be addressed satisfactorily. On each, a seller may acquiesce, compromise or prevail. What's essential is knowing these points and your position beforehand.

## EYES ON THE HORIZON

The point of negotiations is to agree on the myriad terms of a sale. At first glance this is a long list, and the idea of negotiating a purchase agreement can be overwhelming. But to be an effective negotiator, a seller should look beyond the mountain of details to the horizon and outline of the whole transaction. In a microcosmic way it's like building a company. One service, one product, one contract, one dollar, one hurdle at a time, and soon you're looking back over an entire business.

This approach leads to a useful strategy: Leave the relatively minor elements of a sale (although they may be the most emotionally charged) to last. Adroit negotiators, instead of jumping on such questions as the duration of a noncompete and whether the seller's new title will be chief executive officer or chief operating officer, sidle up to the major points first. They focus on the purchase price and how it can be arranged, tackling questions such as the number of years in an installment sale or how stock will be valued or how much money will be held in escrow.

## LIMBERING UP

> "I learned very quickly that I probably should just sit back in my chair and be quiet. Let the Lehman partner do the negotiations. That was one of my smarter decisions. I was in good hands."
>
> —Bill Lennartz

Buyer and seller first decide the mechanics: where to meet, who will be there, and what timetables or deadlines can be met. These decisions are not inconsequential, although they shouldn't be belabored. In considering where, a seller needs to feel on an equal footing with a buyer and avoid any feeling of being placed at a physical or psychological disadvantage by the buyer's people.

A common meeting ground is a lawyer's offices, although that raises the question of whose lawyer. Law offices can suggest the wrong tone for early talks—details get too legal too quickly. Although either the buyer's or seller's offices may be convenient, for reasons of confidentiality negotiators may prefer a less obvious gathering spot. Negotiations can move around: buyer comes to the seller's office, seller visits buyer, both sides meet somewhere in between.

At some point a perceptive seller visits the buyer's office for a look around and a sense of how this person operates. Surroundings, even business offices, mirror individuals, and a seller can glean impressions about a counterpart's motivations and values.

Neutral turf is best. Here neither side can pressure the other through control of the physical setting. In tense negotiations little things such as having a secretary available for immediate typing can give one side an edge. Hotel suites, country clubs and restaurants are neutral turf.

"Who?" is more important than "Where?" Sellers employ different negotiating styles. Some start out alone—one-on-one with the buyer—then call in lawyers to draft clauses and accountants to crunch numbers after main points have been worked out. If a seller is an experienced deal maker, he or she may prefer to negotiate alone and be decisive, creative and aggressive. This approach won't work if the two sides are not equal in authority. If the buyer's representative cannot make commitments and must defer decisions, the decisive seller is left feeling frustrated and annoyed.

On the other hand, a seller shouldn't feel pressured into on-the-spot decisions. Certainly some issues can be resolved readily. But reserve the option of postponing contentious issues and gaining time with the line, "I'll have to talk to my lawyers about that and get back to you."

A valuable negotiating tactic involves not answering all direct questions. The natural response to a direct question is a direct answer. But sometimes a seller shouldn't respond immediately and instead consider the options and consequences. In situations such as this, the adroit negotiator avoids answering sensitive questions by raising new issues, giving half answers or sidestepping the issue.

Not all sellers can or should negotiate alone. Some sellers cannot be dispassionate about their company, lack the patience to haggle prices or become too emotional. Fortunately, most sellers know instinctively, if not from years of business, whether they are effective traders.

Sellers who know better don't negotiate by themselves. They use investment bankers, lawyers, accountants or another business person to bargain for them. Negotiators may be an associate or someone else within the selling company. A seller may not want to sit in on all negotiations but be available nearby for the surrogate to discuss what is happening.

Two problems arise with surrogates. An outside lawyer or accountant may, in the process of negotiation, be pricing the seller's business—making decisions about components of the price. Often, their ideas on price are influenced and inflated by comparisons with public company sales. Such outside negotiators may push too hard for an unrealistic price. Pricing is the seller's arena—an immutable fact surrogates must understand.

The other pitfall with a surrogate is sending the wrong signal to the buyer. A surrogate can be used to stall talks or put off making decisions. This person does not have decision-making authority. If a buyer interprets this person as a weak substitute for the seller, negotiations may disintegrate.

Some sellers prefer a string of advisors at their side—financial vice president, corporate accountant, investment banker and the ubiquitous lawyer. The team approach has advantages, lending itself to the good guy/bad guy routine. (It's easy to imagine: Seller reacts to an offer with an angry outburst and stomps from the room. The buyer, taken aback by the temper tantrum, seeks a compromise more to the liking of the remaining negotiators.) A team presents an array of personalities to interact with the buyer, improving the odds for good chemistry and smooth talks. When deploying the team, sellers should make sure each negotiator has a defined position, whether it be good guy/bad guy, lead negotiator, tactician or observer.

Large groups can be inhibiting. People talk more freely and

openly, and can be more persuasive, in a small group. Lots of listeners make people tentative. Consequently, experienced negotiators usually start with small groups and enlarge the meetings as both sides become more familiar with each other and come to terms.

Another downside to team negotiating is the proverbial too-many-cooks-spoil-the-stew. Too many voices and too many opinions can tear apart a deal at the same time a seller is constructing it. Lawyers may needlessly raise objections when they should be figuring out how to push the proceedings along.

In these early sessions a negotiator communicates to the buyer a positive spirit of cooperation and willingness. The seller must come across as wanting the deal and believing it can be done. Negotiations in the weeks and months ahead will test each person's patience, artfulness and adroitness. A sincere commitment to the transaction will help everyone traverse rough terrain.

"When?" is no small consideration, particularly for the seller. A company is in limbo during negotiations. Generally a seller should talk to just one buyer if they are making progress. The future is on hold until people know who will be running the company. Although employees may not know about a sale until a seller signs a letter of intent and announces it, top management may be very aware. Delays are costly, as balance sheet values or stock prices change and top management focuses on the sale rather than company operations. As a "going concern," any business is always in flux. Suspending its motion, forcing it to tread water, as happens during negotiations, can be harmful. Consequently, sellers should establish a timetable or deadline for completing talks.

## ONE SELLER'S STORY: Bachman Design, Inc.

Tim Bachman sold a graphic design firm in Columbus, Ohio, and vividly remembers his first negotiating session. It was right after an office Halloween party (he and the buyer occupied separate floors of the same building) and right after he heard he was going to be a father.

"It was probably a bit of a pressure play," he recounts. "They had just started their own graphic group and were more or less mimicking what I was doing, which left me with very few new clients. On top of that, I had just learned that my wife was expecting twins. Psychologically, that had a lot to do with it. I started thinking about the stability thing. And the way the offer was made, it was very safe for me. I would still be earning what I was earning, the benefits were better, and it totally eliminated all the hassles of marketing."

Bachman Design, Inc., and its would-be buyer, Retail Planning Associates, circled each other for months. Their design work complemented each other and they shared many accounts. The chief executive officer of Retail Planning, a long-standing acquaintance of Bachman's, made his intentions clear from the beginning of their association. Bachman recalls, "They said anytime I'm ready to let them know. It was mutually understood that the sale was a possibility, but I didn't encourage it at the time."

Ripe for selling, Bachman listened intently to the Halloween party offer. Retail Planning Associates wanted to pay book value for the stock of Bachman Design and give Tim a generous employment contract. Furthermore, Retail Planning's parent company was about to go public, and some of its stock would be included in the pot.

Buyer and seller met again in November. "Handshake time," Bachman calls it. He prepared a list of points to negotiate: his title in the new company, value of furniture, which employees would stay on and at what salary, what clients Bachman would bring with him and their billings, and whether he could carry over royalties from existing accounts.

Although the two sides didn't fix on the exact purchase price, they agreed to base it on book value. At the time Bachman Design was grossing about $800,000, showing a book value around $120,000 and exhibiting "a good-looking balance sheet." Bachman explains the pricing: "It was going to be book value plus a stock option plus salary plus what clients I could bring in and be paid a marketing fee. As it turned out, a lot of the clients were really some of theirs that I had nurtured along and created more work from. Eventually, with a lot of them it was a wash as to whose client they were. It's difficult in the service business to assign value to some of these things."

Critical issues to Bachman were his title, the noncompete clause, and how long negotiations lasted. He hoped to complete the sale by the end of the year. But he didn't make his wishes part of a written understanding with the buyer, so when unexpected delays stretched closing into May they cost Bachman dearly.

Bachman enthusiastically prepared a business plan for how the two firms would integrate employees, projects and marketing. He expected to implement it as an executive in the new entity, but his efforts had an unforeseen downside. "I spent quite a bit of time rewriting my business plan with their group factored in," he remembers. "That became a very ambitious project, which took me away from my business for a couple of months. It resulted in no profit for those months."

While Bachman Design was treading water the buyer became distracted by other ventures, particularly the public offering. "It wasn't that they were trying to put me off," Bachman explains. "They had bigger things on their plate so they put me on the back burner." The public offering not only stalled negotiations but also meant that Bachman had a new chairman to negotiate with.

Talks dragged on for months as Bachman met with the chief executive officers of both Retail Planning and its holding company, Meret, Inc. When he had a financial question he called the chief financial officer of Meret. Bachman frequently negotiated by himself with a Retail Planning executive experienced in acquisitions. It was not an equal match. "Like any kind of negotiations it was one person against a much more sophisticated team," he points out. "But I still felt the opportunities were there."

Debate centered on the noncompete clause. Bachman's attorney advised him not to sign it, believing it limited him too much should his job not work out. Bachman relates, "The buyer was very adamant. All of its executives had one and they couldn't make an exception for me. I was at a more intuitive level. If I was worried about the thing not working, why bother? I felt strongly that it was going to work. If worse came to worse and conditions got so bad that I had to leave, I thought the noncompete would probably negate itself."

Bachman's attorney joined some negotiations, and Bachman was glad for the voice of experience. "He opened my eyes to some values I had that I didn't realize. For instance, I had an extensive slide library that was valuable to them for marketing."

The sale closed in May 1986. Electing for a stock swap to avoid taxes, Tim Bachman received $128,000 in Meret, Inc., stock. The total amount of stock was keyed to Bachman's accounts receivable.

To his dismay, the book value of his company had declined $50,000 from when the sale was discussed in principle in the fall. He concludes, "I'm a little angry that the whole thing was not nailed down better, because of what I lost in book value between October and May. I should have set firmer dates for things to happen and penalties for it not happening. If it wasn't done by a certain time I would want a reconciliation for my time."

## PLAYS FROM THE SIDELINES: DUE DILIGENCE

"I don't think I've ever done a more complicated deal. I had two firms of lawyers, one from Phoenix and one from Orlando. The due diligence they put on us was absolutely unbelievable. Fortune 500 companies are that way, I guess. . . . They wanted copies of every contract, everything that was filed, insurance, and so on."    —Jim Monaghan

Between signing the letter of intent and closing day, the buyer may perform **due diligence** and investigate every aspect of a selling company. Frequently, due diligence moves concurrently with negotiations. The due diligence team, usually business people, lawyers and accountants from the buyer's company, feeds findings to the negotiation team. If the seller's company is large or in a business with which the buyer has no experience the buyer may hire outside evaluators to ensure an independent assessment of its financial condition.

Not all buyers carry out due diligence. Some are hip shooters: they quickly decide to buy, and close immediately. So a seller should not volunteer or invite due diligence, but wait for the buyer to initiate it.

Due diligence discoveries significantly influence prices and terms. This creates shifting sands for negotiators. Points agreed upon may be raised again or, given new information, a buyer may reverse an earlier position. A discovery involving financial information could affect a company's historical earnings, net worth and pricing. A seller avoids such hazards by eliminating surprises and knowing ahead of time what a buyer will discover.

Assertions made in negotiations must be supportable. Skeletons in the closet—a lawsuit by a former employee, an unpaid tax liability, an unusual method of valuing inventory—must be exposed before negotiations and due diligence.

Buyers investigate five areas of a company: management, business operations, financial condition, accounting systems and legal exposure. The seller's job is to cooperate. If negotiations are progressing, a seller should give the buyer all requested documents and papers, and access to offices, facilities and personnel. At the same time, a seller should monitor what is released.

A caveat to company documents: Ask the buyer to keep information confidential and have both parties maintain a list of all papers the buyer sees or receives. Sharing company secrets can be touchy if the buyer is a competitor. Imagine if a company reveals customer and pricing information to a competitor/buyer, then the sale is delayed for six months while everyone waits for an antitrust ruling from the Department of Justice. In this case, arrange for a staged release of information. Parcel out sensitive information only after the buyer has signed a firm agreement in principle and after regulatory, auditing or other time-consuming hurdles have been cleared.

Be prepared for all sorts of requests. Your buyer is looking for material facts about the company as well as legal documents to assure good and clean title. Here's a list of documents and records a buyer will want to see:

- Legal papers: corporation minutes, bylaws, stock books, bank statements and records
- Legal ownership papers: deeds, bills of sale, property titles and leases (with descriptions of property)
- List of shareholders
- Financial statements (three to five years)
- Loan agreements, liens on assets, leases and other financing arrangements

- Receivables (with age indicated)
- Inventory (age, cost and quantity)
- Open contracts (government, sales, supplier, union, employee)
- Tax returns (three to five years)
- Patents and trademarks
- Client/customer lists
- Catalogues, sales literature and brochures
- Pricing structure and policies
- Insurance policies (health, medical, liability, fire and casualty, equipment, building, workmen's compensation)
- Pension plans, severance agreements
- Bonus and stock option plans, ESOPs
- Government rulings or correspondence
- List of employees, salaries, compensation and organization chart

This information and the entire sphere of due diligence activities are not necessarily limited to the buyer. Any seller accepting stock or debentures in the purchasing corporation should investigate their issuer and feel confident about their financial backing.

## THE FIRST MEETING

At the first meeting buyer and seller test the chemistry and get a feel for how the other thinks and makes decisions (deliberative? spontaneous? instinctive?). Personal chemistry is especially critical if a seller wants to stay on. Personality conflicts can make negotiations unpleasant and unproductive; worse still, they may signal that buyer and seller are incompatible and can't work together either before or after a sale.

If buyer and seller have never met, negotiations usually move ahead slowly as each side learns about the other and shows it knows their business and company values. Through casual conversation, before hard bargaining, each side probes for motives and common ground. The buyer tries to discover a seller's *real* reasons. Though a seller may give understandable, acceptable reasons, a buyer assumes there is more to the story. Is a downturn coming? Does a new competitor threaten? The buyer wonders, "How badly does the seller want out?"

The seller probes, too, listening to the buyer's plans for the company. If the buyer is a public company the smart seller will have done some homework on its operations and other acquisitions. Skillful negotiators listen more than they talk. The seller wonders what the buyer wants most and how badly. Cash flow? Product labels? Return on assets? Return on equity? Key personnel? A buyer may have elaborate, ambitious plans. This means a higher price or more incentives for the seller. The answer to what the buyer wants will not be extracted in a single meeting. And there is no single answer. But a negotiator draws out information at every meeting and begins to piece together the puzzle that makes up the buyer's thoughts and intentions.

Besides "How badly?" the other question on everyone's mind is: "How much?" The purchase price hovers like a hot air balloon looking for a place to land, silent yet visible, an unspoken issue. At first, neither side knows enough to bring it up. Each is still exploring, sizing up one another as individuals, business people and potential coworkers.

Discussion of numbers at the first meeting is usually premature. Buyer and seller need to know more about one another's company. Discussing price is premature until the merchandise has been examined closely. Experienced traders know that talking about money before the company facts is pointless or even misleading. Any figure at this point makes the other side wonder, "Is that a serious offer?" or, "Are they trying to pull a fast one?"

Occasionally, a buyer insists on a figure, and even the fanciest footwork can't avoid the direct question. So just in case, a seller should be prepared to mention a very broad range, but it should be as vague as possible. Even ranges of prices may be more than you want to commit to at this point.

Do a little sparring. Jab and retreat as you discuss values and future earnings and formulas and the myriad topics that pop up as you circle around the question of price. This isn't a recommendation to be coy, but to be cautious and thoughtful. Often the buyer has more negotiating experience. You do not want to talk yourself into a pricing corner that you will regret later.

Without getting to actual figures, the buyer's negotiator may want to show a certain flexibility and reasonableness. So this person raises the question of pricing formulas without a commitment to any particular approach.

## PRICING STRATEGIES: RANGE OR PIVOT POINT?

Enough maneuvering. You don't want to dance around the price question indefinitely. The buyer will probably open talks about the price with the gambit, "How much do you want?" Do not answer this question. Do not get trapped into making a flat answer, which is a typical reaction of the inexperienced negotiator. The first rule of negotiating is to never give your number first. At the same time, present yourself as being reasonable and having given a lot of thought to price and value. You want to find out how much the buyer is willing to pay. Respond with a question about the buyer's intentions and ability to pay or say you need more information about the type of offer before you can structure the deal.

There are lots of ways to negotiate. One school centers on price ranges: Each side has a range and tries to find where they overlap. If a buyer names a figure it most likely is the bottom of the range. The trick here is not simply to discover the buyer's range but to broaden that range—push it up and open the possibility of a higher purchase price. To broaden the buyer's range, a negotiator must learn how the buyer arrived at it. What is the yardstick for valuation: Discounted future cash flow? Return on equity? Gross revenues? Return on assets?

Now the seller's negotiator opens up, talking and asking about valuation formulas and other acquisitions and sales. Find out how the buyer's calculator works—what is being fed into it about your company that is contributing to the buyer's price range? Next, increase values by pointing out hidden or unrecognized assets. Direct the discussion to the buyer's valuation and price range, not to how much you want.

If the buyer's range exceeds yours, you're off and running. But what if the buyer's range is below yours? Don't walk away. Buyers, especially experienced ones, are adept at valuation and negotiation. They know what companies sell for and the market value of your business. Lowballing shouldn't be interpreted as unreasonable and rejected out of hand. It is a starting point. Countless companies have sold for many times the opening offer.

Another school aims at discovering the buyer's pivot point and the underlying message of the prices on either side. Arabs bargain this way. Instead of looking for a range, they try to learn a person's central trading point. Anthropologist Edward T. Hall, in *The Silent Language*, describes the process thus:

> **The principle to be remembered is that instead of each party having a high and a low there is really only one principal point, which lies somewhere in the middle. Much like our latest stock market quotation, this point is determined, not by the two parties, but by the market or the situation. Negotiation, therefore, swings around a central pivot. . . . Above and below the central point there is a series of points which indicate what the two parties feel as they enter the field.**

Here is Hall's description of what happens, adapted for the sale of a computer: "The pivotal point was six thousand dollars, the price that day. Above and below this were four points. Any one of the top four might be the first price asked by the seller. Any one of the lower four represents the first offer made by the prospective buyer."

The hidden or implicit meaning of this code is given opposite each step on the scale below. This meaning is not exact but represents a clue as to the attitudes of the two parties as they bargain:

|  | Dollars (000) | Attitudes of Negotiators |
|---|---|---|
| Seller's Asking Price | 12 or more | Seller completely ignorant of the market |
|  | 10.......... | An insult, arguments and fights, seller doesn't want to sell |

| | | |
|---|---|---|
| | 8.......... | Seller will sell but let's continue bargaining |
| | 7.......... | Seller will sell under market |
| | 6.......... | Pivot Point—Market Price |
| Buyer's | 5.......... | Buyer really wants the computer and will pay over market |
| Asking | | |
| Price | 4.......... | Buyer wants to buy |
| | 2.......... | Arguments and fighting, buyer doesn't want to buy |
| | 1.......... | Buyer ignorant of the value of computers |

Most companies are going concerns. Their values fluctuate day-to-day as business comes and goes. Negotiators keep in mind the possibility of a change in a company's finances. Generally, value swings of less than 5 percent are not considered material. However, an essential element in many companies—contracts—can drastically alter values. Open contracts and the profits and expenses they generate may have a significant impact on a company's net worth. During negotiations a seller has to lay these on the table for the two sides to negotiate their effect on the price.

A second rule of negotiating is, Have a walkaway number and be prepared to follow it. The effective trader can take it or leave it. This person is not indifferent but knows that a transaction is not desirable beyond a certain point. A walkaway number is a hard figure that cannot be chipped away or altered. It's an automatic trigger that signals the termination of talks. Sellers must be immovable on this point. A walkaway figure is not a bluff or excuse to march out of the room to extract a better offer. The exit is sincere.

But it's important to know when the walkaway rule applies most. Make or break issues are raised early, and this is the most practical time for a seller to leave. Halting negotiations later, after people have invested in due diligence and lengthy talks, is much more difficult.

Showing a buyer you can walk away adds weight to a bargaining position. It signals that you are less eager than the buyer and your requirements must be met. The following memorandum was written by a seller who broke off talks early and unequivocally, and sent to key employees who knew about the talks. It explains the necessity of a walkaway figure for even a willing seller and conveys the seller's confidence in his action.

---

INTEROFFICE MEMO
TO: ALL OFFICES
FROM: CSW
SUBJECT: SALE TO ———
DATE: SEPTEMBER 10, 198_

Talks with ——— are terminated.

In some respects, it is too bad it ended this way. For I believe we could have mutually contributed a great deal and that it would have been a successful merger. However, for many reasons the inability to agree on price could have been indicative of other problems to come. Even if we had agreed on pricing, there were many other facets to be clarified and resolved. However, they are good people and that side of it would have been interesting.

Nevertheless, these discussions did produce some big benefits for us. It required that we take a real hard look at ourselves, i.e., what we had and what the future of the company will be.

It was positive and reflected in the decision to respond as we did to their offer.

Now, the important thing is to put this all aside and go ahead with the development of the company. We should pursue the growth of our activities and equity.

All the benefits and strengths we identified can be further developed. We recognize what a good thing we have in the company, and it should be a source of pride and optimism. However, all these assets will not produce anything by themselves. It is up to us to vigorously and energetically exploit them. It requires hard work, mentally and physically, to realize the promising future we see.

In short, what we have here in our company should be made a reality.

---

Negotiations are an opportunity to apply a rule we call The Magic of an Odd Number. This rule says that your figures should be an odd number. Regardless of how you arrived at a price, change it to an odd number. Instead of asking for $1.5 million for goodwill, ask for $1.73 million. Nothing even, nothing rounded off. An odd number implies study, thought and sophisticated calculations.

As with all rules, this one shouldn't be followed slavishly. An experienced, sophisticated negotiator might easily see through the odd-number ruse, especially if it seems to jump from thin air. So be prepared to back it up. Book value multiples, P/E ratios and inventory values are useful for arriving at odd figures. If you have no justification, answering a request to explain an odd number could be awkward.

Negotiations are a contest. They're sparring, they're fancy footwork, they're flexing muscles, they're jabbing and retreating. As in the decathlon, more than one person can win any given event. Both sides can get what they want. Enter into talks with a spirit of shared goals and mutual trust. The seller and buyer are not opponents or enemies. They're potential partners, and negotiation is the beginning of that partnership.

## ONE SELLER'S STORY: Eastern Software Distributors, Inc.

Both buyer and seller applied classic strategies and techniques in the sale of a Baltimore company, Eastern Software Distributors, Inc. When a buyer approached owner Shannon Edwards he hadn't thought about selling. "We weren't even looking for a buyer," he recalls. "The buyer came looking for a company to help diversify its operations, so one day I got a phone call from Concord Fabrics wanting to know if they could come down and look at us."

The president and financial vice president of Concord Fabrics visited Eastern Software's offices, a converted house outside the city center where Edwards and twenty employees had worked since 1981. Owned by Edwards and a partner, Eastern Software was grossing about $6 million a year, showing after-tax profits around 4 percent and reporting retained earnings around $230,000. A few days after the tour, the buyer repeated its interest and invited Edwards to New York for negotiations.

Edwards warmed to the notion of selling. He explains, "We knew the industry was getting very crowded. And we knew that times were going to get rough, especially in distribution because it's so easy to get started you can do it at home. It takes a lot of heavy financing to run a business like this and very little profits and return. The risk is higher than the rewards. We thought maybe it'd be best to sell and get out."

Edwards went to New York alone. "My partner decided not to go so there would be some mystique with Concord not knowing who he was," he relates. A silent partner in the background gave Edwards a foil to his demands—a tough, perhaps intractable associate who insisted on certain concessions.

The negotiating session was not pleasant for Edwards. He was on one side of the table and seven or eight people for the buyer were on the other side. After introductions and a few friendly questions the buyer turned on the pressure. "They started firing questions at me from all angles," he recalls. "They were asking all kinds of questions with three of them asking at the same time. It got to the point where I didn't feel like answering any of them. It was like a grilling.

"A major stockholder wanted to know how much I wanted for the business. I said, 'How much are you willing to spend?' They wouldn't give me an answer but wanted to know what I wanted.

"So I said, 'I want two million bucks.' I had no rationale for saying that. It was about nine times earnings over the past three years. So I figured that would get them to move one way or the other. The fellow who asked the question blew up. Had a temper tantrum. He didn't like the figure. Then the president jumped in as if to 'save' me and apologized. He turned to his own man and said I shouldn't have to revise my figure then and there, that it wasn't fair. They were doing good guy/bad guy." Edwards left the meeting thinking, "These guys are going to have to make an offer that is worthwhile . . . at least substantially more than the business had in retained earnings."

A potential tax liability influenced negotiation terms. "We knew that was a skeleton in the closet, so we told them up front and assumed the responsibility," Edwards recounts. "It was a mess— we had both outstanding liabilities and tax credits. The problem arose when the company was started. We ended up with three tax I.D.s. The IRS was tearing its hair out, trying to figure out what we had done. They had money belonging in one account in another account, and back and forth." Because of the messy liabilities, the buyer wanted to purchase only assets.

Days later, the buyer telephoned with a counteroffer: $500,000. Edwards rejected it, but he knew they were close. "I talked it over with my partner and we decided that anything from $750,000 to one million was an equitable price. My partner knew the risks of the business and he figured that the best thing to do was sell at a 'decent' price. Maybe not a fair market price, but a decent price." The two sides Ping-Ponged back and forth, inching closer and closer. They met at $825,000.

Negotiating the price for Eastern Software was just the first round. Buyer and seller struggled over other clauses in the purchase agreement. Negotiations hinged on satisfying Edwards's tough partner. "There were times when it was quite irritating, when people wouldn't agree on certain parts of the contract, when we were stalemated," Edwards reports. "My partner decided that if it didn't go the way he wanted it, it was going to fall through and he didn't care."

Buyers may demand warranties from a seller—guarantees about a company's financial condition and liabilities that may crop up in the future. These are so basic to an agreement that a seller's refusal to make warranties can be an automatic deal breaker. But as the sale of Eastern Software demonstrates, no two transactions are alike and norms are routinely defied.

Edwards continues: "There were certain things he [the partner] was not going to warrant. He didn't want to warrant the truth and accuracy of the financial statements. They were reviewed statements, not audited statements, and he wasn't going to guarantee they were totally factual. They were so close to true it wasn't funny. But if they were off by even 5 percent, then that was it. Finally, they looked at our books carefully and agreed that we were not far off."

Negotiations were not one-sided. Although Edwards and his partner would not warrant the financials, they agreed that the buyer would deposit into escrow the portion of the purchase price representing receivables and inventory. To collect, Edwards had to sell inventory and collect receivables within two years and present the new owner with receipts. "They wanted to see that the business was clean when they bought it, that there were no skeletons in accounts receivable and not a lot of dead inventory," Edwards explains.

Edwards believes that he and his partner negotiated the best possible deal. "The day after it was sold, the industry turned a little bit and it started to get rough. It was to our advantage to sell, whether we knew what was happening or were guessing. The timing was perfect."

## MOVING THROUGH A DEADLOCK

"Everybody sort of blew up over a million-dollar point. We were upset and very close to walking out. The lawyers got us back together again."
—Bud Pearson

Many sales hit a deadlock. Usually it is a temporary obstacle, a moment when both sides must step back to rethink their positions. Deadlocks can bring out the worst in people—stubbornness, bullying, pettiness, irrationality. It's best to resolve them as soon as they arise, before people say things they will regret and do lasting damage.

One way to avoid a stalemate in early talks is to skirt relatively minor points. Too many details too soon create snags. Buyer and seller should strive for a general consensus, an agreement in prin-

ciple before tackling stickier, smaller issues. Ease into larger questions such as price and terms first and leave issues such as employment
contracts, salaries and earn-out clauses until later.

When deadlocks crop up further into negotiations, they can
be handled in the opposite way. Disagreements over major points
should be temporarily put aside so negotiators can debate and
resolve minor points. A series of small victories in the midst of a
larger dispute shows that people are reasonable and reestablishes
feelings of goodwill and willingness. Solving small hang-ups makes
everyone see they can find compromises.

If you reach a deadlock examine its cause. Break it down to
dollars and cents, factor in the number of years involved—how
long you've owned a company or how long a note will run or
whatever—and figure its time-valued worth. For instance, a dispute over $100,000 in a $2 million sale to be paid off in five years
breaks down to 1 percent a year ($100,000 = 5 percent of $2
million, divided by 5 years). Is a sale worth jeopardizing for this
amount? Deadlocks over job titles, noncompete clauses, valuing
stock and other thorny issues can be dissected similarly.

An absolute rule of deadlocks is Don't Lose Your Temper.
Regardless of how frustrating or how infuriating the people, keep
your cool. A blowup or angry argument does irreparable damage.
It offends people and makes them wonder if they can work with
someone who loses control. And assuming the instigator apologizes,
it puts him or her in an awkward, weaker position. (This rule
doesn't contradict the usefulness of good guy/bad guy. The difference is timing and control. A negotiator resorting to good guy/bad
guy has weighed how an outburst will affect another negotiator and
uses this ploy after people are comfortable with and confident of
each other's reactions. But using this routine at a first meeting is
risky.)

Never criticize a buyer, a company or anyone's negotiating
tactics. Criticism does not gain an upper hand and it makes other
people defensive. Sniping or derogatory remarks do not bring negotiations any closer to completion. They impede progress and
threaten a sale.

The flip side of Don't Lose Your Temper is Interject Humor.
The CEO of a San Francisco consulting firm used what sounded

like a ridiculous joke to resolve a $200,000 dispute. Over the course of three meetings, buyer and seller dickered over the value of an apartment the company used for out-of-town clients. The price for the entire company would exceed $11 million, but they could not agree on this apartment and its furnishings. After hours of breaking down costs and assessing similar property values, the seller made a novel suggestion: flip a coin. The buyer chuckled and smiled, "I can't flip for that kind of money." They never flipped, but the suggestion relieved the tension and interjected a bit of playfulness into the room.

Any humor helps. Self-deprecatory remarks, pointing out absurdities, light comments about the evils of money—anything to keep the atmosphere relaxed and friendly. Humor is also a face-saving device. Negotiators backed into a corner with a position or demand they can't support may leverage themselves out with a joke or quip. If you can't pull out humor and are stalemated, halt the talks. Go for a coffee break or out to dinner. Don't hammer at the deadlock unremittingly. Take a day off. Buyer and seller should separate for a few hours or a day or so, get away from each other and the source of the conflict. When negotiations resume they will have fresh insights and new approaches.

# THE SHAPE AND COLOR OF MONEY

Your sale has to be structured. These are the pieces that make up a purchase price: cash, notes, stock, earn-out or combinations of these, and a timetable for paying them. Structure also involves decisions that define the sale legally. And it includes the strategies buyer and seller apply to minimize the tax bite. Structure is certainly part of negotiations, but if you and a buyer are discussing the payout you are advancing beyond *whether* a sale will happen to *how*.

The structure of your sale can be tantalizing. All those choices —money in a rainbow of possibilities. A buyer can pay for your company dozens of ways. As you weigh them, keep in mind the source of the financing and with whom you're dealing. All the choices are contingent on the buyer's ability to pay. A shrewd seller checks out a buyer and knows what the currency is worth. If an offer is for all cash there's little worry. But many sales involve stock or notes, and this is where a seller has to know a buyer and the value of currencies.

## ONE SELLER'S STORY: H. R. Plate and Company

The acquisition world is full of stories about sellers who took a buyer's stock and later pocketed millions or ended with nothing. The eventual outcome is dramatic one way or the other, and in hindsight people wonder if it could have been anticipated. Is there any way to tell how a buyer's stock will perform? Bob Plate could have been more careful and might have protected himself better from his acquired stock's collapse.

San Francisco-based H. R. Plate and Company was a retail food brokerage firm—the classic middleman between food manufacturers and food consumers. Established in 1957, the company had accounts up and down California and represented such national brands as Stokley-Van Camp, Sun-Maid, Alpo Dog Food and Ocean Spray.

As a service business, revenues came from commissions, and gross income was about $500,000. Retained earnings were minimal, enough to cover a few months' expenses. Just before the subject of selling popped up, the firm had a setback with its Gatorade account. It had projected huge sales, then watched the market vanish when the Food and Drug Administration banned one of Gatorade's ingredients, cyclamates. When a buyer appeared, H. R. Plate was straining to meet the additional overhead and travel demands of a new office in southern California.

Plate dreamed of creating a brokerage network from San Francisco to the Mexican border. Teaming with another company could give his company sufficient financing to make it come true.

Plate was introduced to the buyer, Harrell International, through a big client. An interested listener, Plate flew to New York to meet with the president. He recalls, "It looked good. He believed in a lot of the concepts I had. He could offer a much stronger financial base for expansion and take over all the nonproductive functions a food broker has, such as car leasing, payroll, insurance, and leave the broker to do the selling."

Plate returned to California and prepared for the sale. He called other traders in the industry to ask about his suitor. Through sales to military installations, Harrell International had become the world's largest food broker, and at the same time it was garnering a "tremendous reputation" in the industry, Plate recalls. All around him Plate saw green lights.

Before negotiations Plate calculated his company's worth. "Establishing a value for a service business is very difficult," he explains. "You're not talking bricks and mortar, you're not necessarily talking value as a multiple of earnings. Most brokerage businesses are sold on a factor times gross income. Either 1 or 1.5 or 2 times gross income. A lot of times in a private business you can't just look at the bottom-line profit, because the owner purposely is not showing any profit in order to put off taxes. So the surpluses are buried in expense accounts and bonuses and whatever else."

He continues, "I tried to get two times gross income, but the profits weren't sufficient to justify that." They agreed to value H. R. Plate at one times gross earnings.

The two sides, while agreeing to a purchase price around $500,000, traded back and forth over other points. "I had a few things I wanted to include in my employment contract and the buy agreement," Plate says. "I wanted a certain amount of cash equal to the retained earnings and asset value of the company—mostly desks and typewriters." The remainder of the purchase price, around 90 percent, would be paid in the buyer's stock.

"I took stock in Harrell International, a public corporation traded over-the-counter with very little value. But he was putting a higher value on the stock," Plate ruefully remembers. "He was doing blue sky stuff, which I accepted and didn't pay a hell of a lot of attention to. I did make sure that I anticipated wanting to sell some stock to pay back loans, so that took a little dickering. In case I wanted to sell 5,000 shares back to the corporation, it would be at such and such a value. They agreed to that and a year later I exercised it."

Plate negotiated alone, bringing in an accountant and lawyer only for technical advice. He knew the dangers of taking stock. He admits, "It was a risk, but I still was able to increase the salary I was drawing every year. It looked as if it was going to be a very worthwhile investment."

Legally, the sale was a **triangular merger**, with Plate folding his stock into a subsidiary of the buyer. Buyer and seller dissolved their corporations and transferred accounts to a new third company. Plate liked the arrangement, especially the autonomy. "I felt real comfortable with being part of that operation," he remembers. "I had never been in the company fold. I had always been on my own. After selling my business and being a subsidiary, I was still president and ran it as if it were my own."

Three years after the sale Plate sensed trouble. The parent company was grossing more than $14 million but reporting operating losses, he says. "Something was going on," he concludes. By the time his employment contract expired, Harrell International was going out of business and giving food brokers a chance to buy back their companies. Plate proposed purchasing his company with Harrell International stock. He was rebuffed and left holding worthless securities.

With the wisdom of hindsight Plate would have structured the deal differently. He says wistfully, "I would have tried to get a guaranteed value for the stock I kept. I had a guaranteed value for about 20 percent. I should have tried to get a guaranteed value for the balance instead of accepting the blue sky—what we were going to create and build in ten years and the $40 a share value. . . .

"Taking stock depends completely on the company you're selling to. If you've got a Quaker Oats or a ConAgra, then obviously you have a good base for considering taking the stock. There are other considerations, of course—the yield, future growth, whatever. When you're talking about a small over-the-counter company, then it's a different consideration. I would be a lot more wary."

## PROCEED WITH CAUTION

In devising a payment structure you will share confidential information—facts about finances, taxes, pricing and marketing you wouldn't want a competitor or outsider to know. Before diving into the nitty-gritty, draw up a nondisclosure agreement for the buyer. The nondisclosure protects a seller and reassures a buyer. It specifically relates only to confidential, proprietary facts revealed by the seller and not to information discovered during due diligence. The agreement that follows is a sample. Depending on the type of a business, the confidentiality agreement may be much longer and more complex.

[SAMPLE NONDISCLOSURE AGREEMENT]

### NONDISCLOSURE AGREEMENT

(*BUYER company name*) acknowledges that you and your personnel are disclosing to BUYER various business and technical information concerning (*SELLER company name*). Such information may consist of technological information, financial statements, supplier and customer lists and information.

BUYER agrees to hold such information in confidence and will disclose such information only to BUYER'S own personnel and representatives on a need-to-know basis.

If no transaction results between us, BUYER will (a) return to you or destroy all written information provided by you to BUYER and (b) not disclose to any third parties proprietary information furnished by you to BUYER.

BUYER'S obligations under this nondisclosure agreement shall not apply to any information that (a) at the time of the disclosure has been previously published or can reasonably be considered part of the public domain; (b) after disclosure through no act or failure to act by BUYER, becomes part of the public domain by publication or otherwise; (c) prior to disclosure, was known to BUYER; (d) subsequent to disclosure is obtained by BUYER from a third person; or (e) subsequent to disclosure is obtained or developed by BUYER through independent research without use of the disclosed information.

Buyer and Company

Date: _____

## CASH RULES, NOTES FOLLOW

> "I know from my ten-year note that I don't have to worry about finding
> a job next week."                                          —Ken Rothman

Payment comes in four varieties: cash, notes, stock and earn-out.
A buyer offers one or a combination, and in the hierarchy of
currencies cash is king. It won't lose face value, default or be
whipsawed by Wall Street. An all-cash payment enables a seller to
make a complete, clean break with a company and the buyer. It
turns years of work into money for retirement, an estate or post-
poned hobbies. Payment other than all cash has strings attached,
binding buyer and seller together until accounts are settled, which
may take years.

Cash has another appeal. A seller may convince a buyer to
add a premium because of the immediate tax liability raised by all
cash. Imagine the common situation of a buyer with a lump of
money earmarked for acquisitions and a willing seller who wants
to defer taxes but has no place to invest the proceeds. Such a
person could argue persuasively that accepting cash imposes additional expenses, so the purchase price should be upped.

*Cash is not trouble-free.* It raises an immediate tax liability, especially for a seller with a low tax basis in the stock, such as an
owner of a family corporation that began with a small investment.
Cash demands attention; it's an immediate and major investment
concern. A seller has to do something with it—park it in a money
fund, invest it, dole it out to relatives. Sellers unfamiliar with
investment options may find cash a headache.

Cash is often supplemented with **promissory notes**. Notes can
be both risky and rewarding, depending on who issues them and
their terms. And they can work to the advantage of both sides. But
cautious sellers don't want all notes, fearing a buyer may default
or the interest will be less than what they could earn elsewhere.
However, paper from some buyers—blue chip companies with a

long record of servicing debts—is as good as cash. The less solid the buyer, the less secure the notes.

A seller should accept only notes issued by the buyer's parent company and not obligations of a subsidiary, unless the offspring is equally large and financially sound. You want obligations from the strongest, most financially stable issuer, even if this means dealing with parent companies or financial institutions backing a purchase. Grade the paper you're getting. Assess the financial quality of the issuer and its debt history.

A seller worried about the financial backing of a note issuer can negotiate for secured paper. A buyer may back up notes with a mortgage or pledge of assets. Or a seller can ask that purchased stock be deposited in an escrow account until notes are paid. If the buyer reneges on the notes, the seller gets the stock and company back. Another type of security is a covenant in the purchase agreement requiring a buyer to keep the company intact and financially healthy. This covenant guards against a buyer milking a company, defaulting on the notes and then handing back to the seller a worthless shell.

Notes can offer a way for a seller to defer taxes. If a sale involves mostly notes it falls into the category of installment sale. Such a sale puts off taxes until notes are paid, not in the year the sale took place. (More on installment sales later.) While notes create two tax liabilities—for the principal and the interest—they can be arranged to come due when a seller is best prepared to pay them.

A seller taking notes should negotiate for a higher purchase price to compensate for the additional liabilities and risk. Sales composed of notes generally demand a higher price than an all-cash deal. How much higher? Hard to say. No one would argue that $1 million cash is worth the same as $1 million in notes.

Interest on the notes compensates for part of the added risk. Rates are tied to the prime rate, Treasury bills or other interest-sensitive investments and either move with them or are fixed. Prime pays the highest variable return, especially from a major bank. Prime rates at smaller banks may be less. Regardless, interest on notes should exceed returns on government securities or other relatively risk-free instruments.

Another important feature of notes is whether a seller is free to sell or trade them to a third party. It's not uncommon for a buyer to assume automatically the notes will be non-negotiable. Buyers prefer sellers to hold on to their paper because if something goes wrong with a sale they can then withhold payment. So a seller bargains for negotiable notes.

A willingness to accept notes can make a sale more workable. A deal may not be accomplished unless the buyer can supplement cash with an IOU. Some sellers prefer notes to all cash, regarding the regular payments as a steady income. They take part of the purchase price in notes so interest generates income while they figure out what to do next. Notes help sellers regulate a flow of money until they are prepared to manage and invest it.

Another variety of currency is **convertible debentures**, a hybrid of notes and stock. These notes pay interest and can be exchanged for the buyer's common stock if it reaches a specified price. This currency is safer than common stock and has the added incentive of enabling a holder to collect more if the buyer's stock goes up. A seller taking convertible debentures asks two questions: At what price can they be exchanged and at what ratio—how many convertible debentures equal one share of stock?

## GAMBLING WITH STOCK

Stock raises a tantalizing question: Should a seller accept a buyer's stock on the chance it will rise or play it safe and take cash? Stock binds a seller to the buyer and can be a strong incentive for executives to stay with the buyer's business. And taking stock can make a deal happen.

Stock has the added allure of generally being a tax-free or tax-deferred currency because taxes are due when the certificates are sold. The exception to this tax-free feature is when a seller receives property, bonds or debentures in addition to the stock. This excess amount, called **boot**, can be expensive for a seller. These noncash extras create an immediate tax bill. Kinds of boot a buyer may chip in when paying with stock are investment or estate planning advice, an option to buy related property from the seller, rights to purchase more common stock, and allowing puts and calls to be attached to stock.

*Accepting a buyer's stock is an investment decision, not a selling decision.*  A seller is gambling on the stock market, on an individual industry and on the buyer's company. A buyer's equities pose the same questions as any stock purchase: Is the current price reasonable? What's the earnings growth potential? Does the stock pay a dividend? Judge a buyer's stock by the same criteria applied to all common stock.

Some equities are better investments than others. Common stock of a large company with a history of earnings, dividends, manageable debt and market demand is safer than that of a new company with no earnings and no dividend which is betting on the future. Stock in a new growth company may appeal to a seller who remains with a company and can monitor it.

A seller's opinion of stock may be influenced by restrictions imposed by a buyer or the SEC or by the kind of stock. Stock may be common or preferred and registered, exempt from registration or "shelf" registered.

Common stock and preferred stock are valued differently. Common is valued according to market price. The value of preferred and its dividend are negotiable. Preferred stock is safer— less subject to market swings—but also less likely to show dramatic gains. Whether common or preferred, the stock has to carry voting rights. Otherwise, gains from the exchange are taxable.

A third currency is **convertible preferred stock**. These shares can be converted to a company's common when it hits a certain price. This is having your cake and eating it, too. It extends the safety of preferred stock (if a company goes under, preferred shareholders are in front of common shareholders) and the potential reward of a climbing common stock. Like preferred stock, these shares can pay regular dividends.

Stock is either registered with the SEC or exempted from registration. If registered, the company has filed disclosure forms with the SEC. Registration is time-consuming and expensive, unless the company is large and makes regular public offerings. Sometimes buyers offer "**shelf**" **registered stock**. This paper is "on the shelf" at the SEC, immediately available for registration and sale as long as a company trades it within two years.

In an acquisition with few sellers and a relatively small amount of stock, a buyer may not want the inconvenience or expense of registering stock. So **unregistered stock** is put on the table.

Unregistered stock cannot be readily sold or traded. The SEC says that anyone holding this stock cannot sell it for two years, can sell only a small percentage during any three-month period and must notify the SEC when it is sold. The SEC Rule 144 contains numerous "ifs" and "buts." For instance, the notification requirement doesn't apply if the sale involves fewer than 500 shares and less than $10,000.

The most obvious drawback to unregistered stock is not being able to trade it. A seller can't hand it over to a broker and immediately convert it to cash. So in return a seller bargains for compensation—additional shares, future registration rights, higher dividends.

A seller may ask a buyer to **piggyback** unregistered stock. In piggybacking, a seller later adds his or her shares when a buyer is registering a batch for a public offering. In return, a buyer may ask for conditions, such as first rights to buy back unrestricted stock or that an attorney approve any stock sale.

A seller accepting unregistered stock signs an investment letter. (Hence, these shares are sometimes called **restricted** or **lettered stock**.) By signing, a seller agrees to keep the stock as an investment and not sell it for a couple of years or until it is registered. In any consideration of unregistered stock, a seller should enlist the help of a securities attorney.

A seller taking a substantial chunk of a buyer's stock may become an "insider" and subject to trading restrictions regardless of whether the stock is registered. A seller who accepts an executive position with the buyer or a seat on the board of directors is an insider. And insiders are limited as to when they can sell stock.

Stock prices undoubtedly will change between the initial agreement and closing. So buyer and seller concoct a way to price stock.

Here are some ways:

- Fix the price to an average trading price over a certain number of days or peg the price to one particular day.
- Establish an exact number of shares and take your chances: if the stock goes up the purchase price is boosted, and if the market drops the seller loses.
- Establish a minimum and maximum number of shares with the final number determined by the price of the stock on closing day (called a **collar**).
- Agree to average the price range on closing day.

Regardless of the formula, stock prices will shift, adding a casino element to a seller's stock. If the price changes too much before closing and skews the purchase price, the sale may be called off.

## THREE SHAPES OF A SALE

A company can legally be sold one of three ways. These dictate how a buyer reports the purchase on the accounting books, to stockholders and according to state corporation laws.

Here are the choices:

**1.** *Asset Sale:* Buyer purchases title and ownership to seller's assets and assumes liabilities, but not necessarily all assets or all liabilities. Seller may hold on to some. Seller's corporation still exists even though most of the assets are gone. The corporate structure, as well as the stock, of the selling company is unchanged. After an asset sale sellers commonly liquidate their company and distribute the proceeds to stockholders after paying taxes and other liabilities. A sole proprietorship or partnership sells assets.

**2.** *Stock Sale:* Seller and other stockholders sell stock and hand over certificates in the corporation to the buyer. This sale is a transaction between shareholders and the buyer. The selling corporation remains intact—it just has new shareholders.

3. *Merger:*    Called a **statutory merger**, this requires the selling company to merge or combine assets and operations into the buyer's company. Generally, the seller's board of directors and stockholders must approve a merger. The buying company is usually the surviving corporation and, depending on state corporation laws, owns all assets and liabilities. The seller does not transfer titles to individual assets. The selling corporation is dissolved and its stockholders usually trade their shares for shares in the buyer's company.

In today's tax climate a stock sale is preferable because it avoids double taxation. Stockholders are taxed only on their personal gains, not the corporate gain. In an asset sale the corporation is taxed on any gain and shareholders are taxed on the gain in the proceeds they receive over the amount of their stock basis.

## BUYER'S BOOKKEEPING SWAYS PRICES

The purchase of a company appears on the buyer's books one of two ways: as a **pooling of interests** or a purchase. The difference is an accounting distinction that affects the buyer's book value, earnings and stock value. In principle, a seller cares little how a buyer accounts for an acquisition (unless, of course, the seller is taking the buyer's stock). In practice, the buyer's accounting can influence the purchase price and structure of a sale.

In a pooling of interests, a buyer adds the book value of the seller's assets, liabilities and previous year's earnings to the balance sheet. Securities traded in the transaction appear on the buyer's books. Goodwill usually does not appear on the buyer's books. Buyers like to keep goodwill away from financial statements because, unlike other assets, goodwill cannot be amortized and written off. In essence, pooling is a merger between equals and a combining of financial statements.

Buyers, however, cannot randomly choose whether to use pooling or purchase accounting. The transaction dictates how they must account for it. To qualify as a pooling of interests, a sale has to meet certain conditions. These relate to how the buyer's and seller's companies are owned and managed before and after the sale and how payment is structured. The criteria are complicated—the buyer's accountant will know the twists and turns. Nonetheless, sellers should know that usually buyers prefer a pooling of interests in a stock swap. A sale that can qualify for a pooling can increase the value of the transaction for a seller.

When pooling cannot be used the purchase method is applied. The buyer records the actual price paid for an acquisition. The purchase price is frequently greater than the appraised value of the individual assets, and this higher price is what appears on the buyer's books. When a buyer pays more than book or appraised value of the assets, that premium has to be recorded as goodwill. And goodwill is an unwanted entry on balance sheets because it cannot be readily depreciated and written off. This can mean higher taxes and lower reported earnings.

In short, pooling reflects a merger and purchasing reflects an acquisition. The first method does not necessarily reduce a buyer's future earnings and the second method can. And a buyer who wants a pooling badly enough and can qualify, may be willing to pay for it.

## ONE SELLER'S STORY: Madison Financial Services

Dry accounting methods were translated into a personal dilemma when Bill King sold Madison Financial Services. The intricacies of pooling, purchasing, stock registration and restrictions became the focal point of intense debate among King and his partners. Each partner wanted to package the sale differently. Their final compromise was more complicated than their dealings with the buyer.

Bill King and a partner started Madison Financial in Nashville in the late 1960s as an advertising firm serving banks. Their basic product was radio jingles until banking deregulation brought opportunities to expand into full-service checking accounts. When demand for Madison Financial checking packages exceeded requests for radio spots, the firm dropped its advertising business.

King had not thought seriously about selling until Madison's main competitor sold to Comp-U-Card International, a public company in electronic merchandising. Madison's strong financials and market share ensured it a spot on Comp-U-Card's shopping list. King's company, of which he owned 45 percent, was grossing $18 million, with pretax earnings of $5 million and book value around $8 million. Its client list contained 1,400 banks and a 10 percent market share.

Bill King thought he didn't want to sell. He had examined going public and a leveraged buyout and decided against both. He explains, "We had taken the long view of developing the company and were never concerned about maintaining fantastic growth. It happened that we were a very profitable business and showed good margins. We were always inclined to put a lot of money into new product development at the expense of bottom-line profitability. We didn't dress the company up."

The would-be buyer contacted King through the chairman of the company that had just been acquired. King had known him for years, and they had even talked about combining their operations. But, he recalls, both were "fiercely independent, so it never went anywhere. Neither of us wanted to take a secondary role."

Bill King and the chairman of Comp-U-Card were introduced in a New York restaurant. The buyer did most of the talking, describing his company and hopes for the future. "In hearing his vision for the company we became considerably more interested," King reflects. "I learned more about the company. It's characterized as young with very aggressive management. We always thought of our management as young and very aggressive—theirs was even younger. Young, bright guys. Heavily laden, workaholic, sales-oriented people who weren't afraid to try new things."

The matching corporate cultures clearly swayed King. He returned to Nashville and scrutinized his suitor. In a reversal of roles the seller performed due diligence on the buyer. King read annual reports and prospectuses and conferred with financial analysts. "Everything came up positive," he remembers. "We basically liked their style and thought there was an opportunity for greater growth with them than without them."

An important negotiating point for King was his job. While unconcerned about an ironclad employment contract, he wanted a major role. He insisted on an executive, not operating position: "I wasn't ready to retire." Debate about King's position in effect skirted the question of the purchase price until the third meeting.

For that conference, King prepared spreadsheets and calculated Madison's cash growth and earnings. "We sat down and ran through our projections and historical numbers," he relates. "We were all pretty well agreed on the value of the company. It wasn't a major issue. We knew what they paid for Financial Institutional Services and felt that we could justify a somewhat better price based on our recent growth."

With the price settled, the men turned to its structure. King says, "There was a good deal of discussion on how we would do it: all stock, partial stock, partial convertible debenture or partial cash?" At this point the buyer faded from the scene, and King grappled with his partners. "There were probably more negotiations between the three principals of our company than between the principals of the two companies." King explains: "After we overcame 'Do we want to sell?' [which was the secondary obstacle], we hit the primary obstacle, which was 'How do we structure it? Are we willing to take a market risk?' We felt good about Comp-U-Card, but the market was sailing pretty high at that time and we had been a very conservatively managed company since Day One. Never had any corporate debt, had a lot of money in the bank. We weren't comfortable with taking a total market risk.

"We had different visions of risk. It's like marriage counseling —you deal with issues and personal goals and objectives and priorities that have never been raised before. In three people we had one that was totally risk-averse, one totally risk-oriented, and one somewhere in the middle."

The gamble was whether to accept all stock in a pooling-of-interests transaction. Clearly, the buyer preferred a pooling. King recalls, "From a pure earnings per share basis, it would have been more favorable [to the buyer] to do a pooling. If we took all stock we could have taken some that could be registered a reasonable time after the transaction. But we were not inclined to take all stock—we wanted some sort of combination of cash and stock. We decided it would be cleaner to take some restricted stock and a significant amount of cash."

After wrestling with stock versus cash, King and his partners tackled the question of what kind of stock. They opted for restricted, unregistered shares. "We could have registered half of it within a few months, but in order to do that you're taking a risk. Under the pooling-of-interests regulations, you don't have a firm price when you do that. We would have taken our chances with the market price. Everyone we talked to indicated the market was solid, that it was a no-brainer to take stock and get out, but we didn't want the risk." Pricing the stock was comparatively easy: King and the buyer accepted the market price on the day they shook hands on the sale. "We just took our chances," King reflects.

The package totaled $33 million—$15 million cash, $12 million convertible debentures (paying 8 percent over ten years) and $6 million in stock.

For sixty days, buyer and seller inspected each other. King chose this time to inform employees. "We wanted everything done quickly and confidentially because we didn't want it to leak to our people or clients," King explains. "We were very concerned. When we had the handshake we called in six or seven officers Saturday morning to tell them before we announced it on Monday."

King mulled over how the companies would fit. He would be part of the new entity and wanted a clear path for growth and expansion. He wanted, in the buzzword of business school, a synergy.

King says, "We probably spent more time on our due diligence than they did. Our chief financial officer spent lots of time in Stamford going over their books and operations. We wanted to be comfortable with the numbers. We were betting on the future and weren't interested in selling to a company that didn't have a future as good or better than ours. That was the due diligence. If we hadn't seen a vision for the future we would have backed out. We're a sales organization, so we looked at what kind of sales operation they had—what is the universe, what is the market, what services do they have we can incorporate into. It was not a numbers-oriented due diligence."

Closing day for Bill King was no more exciting than a shuttle flight to New York. Everyone gathered at the offices of the buyer's lawyer. King recalls, "We waited for things to be typed up and signed, gave instructions to have the money wired to our money funds and rushed to the airport. We didn't even pop a cork."

King has no regrets about selling. Forty-two years old, "not ready to pull out the golf clubs," and lacking any plans for his newfound wealth ("I made a real conscious effort not to change my life"), he willingly handed over the stock of Madison Financial.

His confidence comes from a feeling that he negotiated a safe yet profitable package. "I would be very sure of your inclination to sell. And accept that it's going to go bad, because then anything that happens is no surprise," he advises. "I've heard horror stories of people who sold their companies for stock and the market went to hell. They took stock worth $36 a share, and nine months later, before they could get it, it was down to $10."

## MINIMIZING TAXES

"I'm tickled pink to pay all the taxes I owe. The more taxes I have, the more money I have. You got to have it to pay it. My accountant told me something I've lived by all my life: 'As long as you can accept that Uncle Sam is going to be your 50 percent silent partner, you'll never have any problem.' "
—Steve Rosendorf

Taxes are always in the back of a seller's mind. There's the obvious question: "How much will I have to pay?" And the less obvious: "Will I have enough cash to pay them?" and "Could taxes obliterate my goals?" and "Can I pay less?" and "Can the buyer help me reduce them?"

Managing taxes, like constructing the sale, is a series of choices and decisions. A seller has many options, each with its own tax ripple. None of the choices is easy. Each has pluses and minuses.

The first question is whether a sale will be taxable or tax-free (not really free, but deferred until another year). Restated, the quandary is, "Pay now or pay later?" An unavoidable conclusion is that a seller will pay taxes sooner or later no matter what. This leads to the crux of the tax debate: How do you reduce these inevitable taxes?

A company that sells for more than its original start-up value generates a tax liability. The sole proprietor who borrowed $5,000 to start a consulting firm, then sold its assets (mainly a client list) five years later for $500,000, faces a tax bill on the $495,000 gain. The shareholders of a fast-growing corporation founded on $3 million of venture capital who sell all their stock for $5 million owe taxes on $2 million.

In a company sale there are two potential tax entities: the individual and the corporation (if a company is unincorporated, there is only the individual). A basic tax strategy for a seller is to elude double taxation—taxes on the corporate level and the personal level. This double taxation is a new worry for many sellers. Until the 1986 Tax Reform Act, most sellers paid only personal taxes if they liquidated their corporation soon after the sale. For fifty years, companies could escape a double tax if they followed the guidelines of the General Utilities Doctrine. The 1986 Tax Act eliminated that doctrine. Today, dodging the double-tax bite has become more difficult.

A company sells either stock or assets. If it sells assets it incurs a tax liability on the appreciated value of each item. Some assets, such as costly buildings or real estate, may have gained little. Others, especially intangibles such as research, patents or market share, have a small initial value and may have appreciated considerably. The maximum federal corporate tax rate on the gain is 34 percent. Add to this a state corporate tax rate that can be significant, such as in California, New York or Wisconsin.

When a company distributes proceeds from an asset sale to shareholders they owe taxes on the gain in their holdings. That individual rate can be as high as 33 percent plus state taxes. Here's a simple example of how double taxation works: The owner of Zippety-Do-Dah Computer Company, which opened its doors ten years ago with a capital investment of $300,000, sells its assets for

$4.3 million. The corporate tax on the gain is $1.36 million (34 percent of $4 million). The state will also tax the transaction, but because rates vary we will omit that additional hit. The corporation then dissolves and distributes the proceeds to the seller. The seller's tax on the gain is $823,200 (28 percent of $2.94 million, the after-tax proceeds).

Sellers can escape double taxation by selling stock instead of assets. In a stock sale only individuals, not the company, owe on the gain in the stock's value. There's only one tax bite in this transaction, making it the choice of most sellers. The biggest obstacle may come from the buyer. A buyer may object to a stock sale because it can increase his taxes. By buying stock instead of assets, a buyer may miss out on being able to increase the tax basis of assets purchased and on acquiring future depreciation that lowers taxes.

In pre-1986 Tax Act days, sellers almost gladly paid taxes. It was the era of long-term capital gains rates. These were a mere 40 percent of the rates applied to ordinary income. For an individual in the 50 percent bracket, that meant a capital gains rate of 20 percent. All gone. Today, both long- and short-term capital gains are taxed at the same level as ordinary income: 28 to 33 percent. The only saving grace is it's less than the 34 percent corporate rate, a strong incentive for sellers to avoid corporate taxes.

## WINDOW OF OPPORTUNITY: OPEN FOR TWO YEARS

The double-tax hit contains a loophole. The 1986 Tax Act opened a two-year window of opportunity for small companies. Until December 31, 1988, small, closely held companies can sell assets and pay only one level of taxes. This exemption is aimed at corporations valued at less than $5 million. If a company sells for less than $5 million and more than half of its stock is owned by ten or fewer people and they have owned this stock for at least five years, the corporation will not be taxed on the sale. If a company sells for $5 million to $10 million, it partially avoids corporate taxation.

Sellers too large to qualify for this exemption may have another choice. Convert into an S Corporation—a vehicle for companies that want the protection and structure of a corporation but the tax treatment of an individual. An S Corporation that sells assets passes the gain (or loss) to individual shareholders who are taxed at their personal rate. There is no tax on the corporate level.

Not everyone can retool into an S Corp. An S Corporation can have no more than thirty-five shareholders, only individuals as shareholders (no investment groups such as Employee Stock Ownership Programs or venture capital firms) and only one kind of voting stock. And for a seller, an S Corp has a hitch: no selling or liquidation within three years (ten years starting in 1989) of conversion, otherwise the IRS will tax it like a regular corporation.

The Tax Act changed another rule that could ricochet and hit sellers. This rule involves a buyer's ability to assume a seller's tax losses. While "net operating loss carryovers" (this is English to accountants) do not directly affect a seller's taxes they can influence a buyer's thinking about the purchase price. In earlier times a buyer merging with a company or purchasing its assets could assume the seller's credits for either past or future tax losses. This provision made a struggling company with substantial losses appealing to a cash-rich buyer looking to reduce its tax bill.

That was the old days. Now a buyer cannot use all of a seller's tax losses. The annual limit is set by a formula, basically a small percentage of the loss. Moreover, to qualify for the loss carryover, a buyer cannot liquidate the seller's business for two years after the sale. In essence, the change in loss carryovers means sellers have one less charm on their bracelet.

When President Reagan signed the Tax Reform Act, he changed the lives of all business sellers. Inevitably, they will pay more taxes. Two ways to dodge the tax man are by selling stock instead of assets and, if possible, reorganizing into an S Corporation. These help avoid the double-tax bite. For a tax-free (read: "tax-deferred") transaction, an earn-out or installment sale is the answer. With these, a seller can put off receiving part of the purchase price until later years.

## BETTING ON TOMORROW: EARN-OUTS

> "You have mixed emotions. You're no longer the boss. I intended to live with it [the buyer] for three years. Work hard for my own good and also build up some reserves for the inside shareholders for any contingencies. My goal was to get them their shooter back in three years. I said that at the end of the three-year period I'd be disappointed if they didn't have all their money back."   —Bud Pearson

An **earn-out** is a great problem solver. It can resolve disagreements over price, bridge differences and move negotiations forward. It can motivate a seller to stay with a company and enlarge earnings. It can help a seller postpone taxes. For a seller staying with a company, an earn-out is as valuable as a reserved parking space.

An earn-out allocates, extends and, in some cases, increases a purchase price. It is additional payment made to a seller based on the future performance of an acquired company. In some sales the earn-out is a portion of the purchase price. A sale may call for an initial payment of 70 percent of the target price and the remainder paid through an earn-out. In other cases an earn-out is gravy—money on top of the basic purchase price and an incentive to a seller.

When an earn-out is part of the purchase price it becomes a practical way to resolve differences about future earnings. A buyer basing the purchase price on earnings potential may differ with the seller's projections. Instead of locking horns over future earnings, a seller can suggest an earn-out. Basically, a seller says, "If you won't pay what I think my company will earn, wait and see. Pay me when the money starts rolling in." A seller offers to defer part of the purchase price to after closing and make it dependent on coming earnings.

The portion of the purchase price generally covered by an earn-out ranges from 20 to 60 percent, and the earn-out period lasts from one to five years. These are common terms, not strict rules. Earn-outs follow no set formulas. Seller and buyer can be as inventive and imaginative as they want in sculpting these arrangements. Whatever works and feels good.

In another scenario, an earn-out constitutes a bonus and incentive on top of the purchase price. A seller agrees to continue working with a company under the new owner and receives additional pay based on company performance. Although a seller may have received the purchase price in full, an incentive earn-out may be a necessity. It may be the only way a buyer can persuade a seller to remain with the company and keep profits flowing.

Despite its attractions an earn-out contains a booby trap. It can create as many if not more problems than it solves. The trap surrounds the question of how an earn-out is calculated. The debate as to what exactly constitutes "earnings" has confounded and rankled many a buyer and seller.

In an earn-out situation the acquired company must separate its financial reporting from the buyer's company. And both parties must agree on how to measure company performance, how the earn-out is paid and contingencies for extraordinary events. Sounds easy, but it's not.

An earn-out can be paid in cash or stock. The face value of cash but not stock is clear. If the currency is to be the buyer's stock the two sides have to value it. Is the stock valued when the earn-out is arranged or years later when earnings figures are in and the value of the shares has risen or fallen? This figuring can be as complex as valuing stock as a component of the purchase price.

The thorniest issue is defining earnings. "Earnings" invariably are a pretax net figure. A seller especially wants to net out or eliminate extra or hidden expenses produced by the acquisition. An acquisition can impose new expenses on a company: finance costs, home office overhead, accounting and auditing, and legal fees. In addition, the new parent company undoubtedly does business differently. This new style may well be translated into new charges for an acquired company. These may involve accounting methods, salaries, taxes, employee bonuses, capital expenditures and depreciation, and noncompetitive purchasing requirements.

It's not enough to agree that an acquired company will follow generally accepted accounting principles. The earnings calculations must be defined exactly. A seller has to know which expenses are going to shave an earn-out.

Establishing what comprises earnings is the first hurdle. The next is the formula for translating these into a payout. There are dozens of earn-out formulas. It's like a gin rummy hand—all sorts of cards make gin. Here are some common ways to structure an earn-out:

> *Base period earnings:* Earn-out equals a percentage of earnings that exceed those of a particular year, often the year of the sale. The base year is used as a constant benchmark, so earnings must exceed only those in the initial period and not annually. Another method fixes the payment as a specific amount rather than a percentage over and above the base year.
>
> *Incremental earnings:* Earn-out equals a percentage (or specific amount) of earnings that exceed those of the previous year. For this system to pay off earnings must increase every year.
>
> *Cumulative earnings:* Earn-out is a percentage (or specific amount) of combined earnings over a number of years. This system allows for earnings that fluctuate and doesn't pay until earnings have accumulated over a set number of years.
>
> *Return on investment:* Earn-out is a percentage of or everything above an established return on assets (also called return on investment). Net income (net has to be defined) is divided by the total value of assets. The resulting percentage indicates how much an acquirer's investment in a company is generating. If the target return on investment is 25 percent the earn-out can equal a percentage of money over and above it.
>
> *Growth in sales or margins:* Earn-out is a percentage of (or specific amount over) a target amount for gross sales or profit margins. Like everything else, what goes into these categories has to be well-understood.

There's a personal catch to an earn-out. It's called, "Who's in charge?" While a remaining seller is responsible for the operations that produce earnings, the new owner may have plans for the company that alter its performance. A seller wants the freedom to run the company as before and generate promised earnings. On the other hand, the buyer may want to shift its activities to suit acquisition purposes. If buyer and seller are at cross-purposes they have to resolve them before an earn-out can work.

## STALLING THE IRS: INSTALLMENT SALES

An **installment sale** defers taxes. Instead of receiving the purchase price in one lump, a seller elects to have it parceled out and receive it over years. The biggest attraction of an installment sale is that it puts off taxes. By spreading the purchase price over future years, a seller owes taxes on gains from the sale only as the cash comes in. The tax liability equals the percentage of the gain from the sale. In a $5 million installment sale that is paid in five equal parts, with a $1 million gain for the seller, yearly taxable income equals 20 percent of the gain. (The risk here for sellers is that tax rates may go up in the future.)

Not all deferred payment schemes are installment sales, according to the IRS. To qualify as an installment sale, part or all of the purchase price must be paid in a year following the year of sale. A nice twist on installment sales is that in a transaction involving more than one seller, some can take this route while others receive their money up front. This mechanism helps accommodate sellers who want to put off investment decisions or, should the purchase amount consist of taxable noncash (e.g., marketable notes), do not have enough cash to pay taxes immediately.

| CHAPTER **8** | # POLISHING THE PURCHASE AGREEMENT |
|---|---|

> "It felt like when my son graduated from high school. My successful company was going on to bigger and better things."  —Dee Weitzel

It's called by a variety of names: purchase agreement, definitive agreement, closing document, acquisition contract, sales contract. Regardless of the title, it's the document that defines your sale, how money will be exchanged and the mechanics for transferring a company. This is where you gather all the conversation and loose talk and put it into concrete, legal language.

The length and crafting of this document vary from sale to sale. It can be one page or hundreds of pages. Shorter versions tend to cover larger stock sales with many shareholders in the selling company. In these, the seller's promises and guarantees, as well as the purchase price, are fairly cut-and-dried. Longer documents emerge from smaller asset sales involving the transfer of numerous assets and liabilities.

A **purchase agreement** involves a balancing act. Imagine a seesaw with each end adjusting its weight to find a safe spot in the middle, thereby balancing risk. The seller discloses everything known about a company and asserts these facts are true. If they later

167

prove to be false part of the purchase money, as well as the deal itself, could be lost.

At the other end, the buyer of a nonpublic company is on largely unfamiliar ground. While a buyer knows much about the target, the target may hold surprises and possibly hidden liabilities. The buyer will be living with the company for a long time and gambles that the company is as the seller presented it: no costly unknown conditions or events lurk around the corner.

So each side attempts to reduce the risk of a failed sale or buying trouble while also accepting the inevitability of some risk.

A purchase agreement goes through few drafts—the fewer the better. Numerous editions with lots of legal nitpicking can sour a sale. Buyer and seller outline major issues in the first writing. The final document could be the second draft with only minor changes.

Usually it's the prerogative of the buyer's lawyers to prepare the agreement. The first draft, with its conditions and clauses and demands, can reveal a buyer's thinking—what's important and what's unimportant. This is useful to a seller in negotiating agreement terms.

However, a seller who believes it's harder to persuade someone to remove than to insert language in a document can offer to write the first draft. Instead of reacting and counterproposing, a seller inserts the best terms and lets the buyer respond. Experienced agreement writers believe it is easier to persuade the other side to add to a contract than to remove material from it.

## BRIEF FORK IN THE ROAD

Virtually every purchase agreement contains a description of and disclosures about what is being sold, the purchase price and how it is calculated and paid, statements of fact and guarantees of the buyer and seller, the mechanics for closing, and supporting documents. But in a few places, agreements differ on whether a sale is a transfer of assets or stock.

Sole proprietorships and partnerships sell assets because they have no stock. But sometimes a corporation sells assets. In an asset sale the agreement specifies the kind of assets being purchased, whether they include current assets such as inventory, merchandise and receivables or fixed assets, and how these are valued. It also identifies which liabilities, if any, are being assumed.

Each kind of asset is valued differently. With current assets, negotiators agree on a basis for valuation (for example, the lower of market or cost), and the final purchase price is determined on closing day by an actual accounting of current assets. This approach allows for last-minute price adjustments for inventory counts and "off balance sheet liabilities," such as obligations for retiree health plans or life insurance. In this instance, the buyer purchases the company's net working capital. For fixed assets, negotiators price the whole collection of plant, equipment and intangibles such as patents, trademarks and goodwill.

In a stock sale stockholders (and spouses if they live in a community property state) agree to relinquish all outstanding shares for cash or other payment. The nature of these shares—number issued, par value if any, class (e.g., voting common stock) and any rights attached—is described fully. The agreement may also list the holdings of each stockholder and what percentage of the company they represent.

In either a stock or asset sale, payment is expressed in dollars, shares of stock or notes, and is accompanied by explanations such as terms for financing, escrow deposits, earn-outs or installment plans, and methods for valuing and registering stock. The agreement also informs the seller of how and when money is exchanged, for instance by wire transfer on closing day to a bank account.

In today's tax climate, stock sales are more popular than asset sales. Asset sellers face the possibility of double taxation (unless the sale is for less than $5 million and happens before January 1989) while selling shareholders are taxed only once on personal gains.

Below is an outline for a purchase agreement for a stock sale. While lawyers use more or less similar forms, they tailor each to the needs and demands of a particular sale. This outline is "untailored," but the following explanation points out where buyer and seller can interject individual features.

STOCK PURCHASE AGREEMENT

   I.  Description of the Sale of Shares
      A.  Name of each shareholder
      B.  Number of shares held by each shareholder
  II.  Purchase Price
      A.  Total payment to shareholders
      B.  Conduct of an audit before closing
      C.  Adjustment to purchase price if book value falls below a certain amount before closing
 III.  Contingent Purchase Price
      A.  Description of an earn-out
      B.  Imputed interest for the earn-out
      C.  Calculations and period of time for the earn-out
  IV.  Pre-Closing Deliveries by Shareholders
      A.  Financial statements
      B.  Disclosure letter
      C.  Power of attorney
   V.  Closing
      A.  Time and place
      B.  Documents to be delivered by shareholders: certificates, corporate records, legal opinion, bank accounts, general release, resignations
      C.  Deliveries by the buyer: cash, legal opinion
  VI.  Representations and Warranties of the Buyer
      A.  Organization and standing of the company
      B.  Authority to execute sale and legally bind the agreement
      C.  Any fees owed to business brokers or finders
 VII.  Representations and Warranties of the Seller
      A.  Title to shares
      B.  Making a valid and binding agreement
      C.  Organization and standing of the company
      D.  Status and number of authorized capital stock
      E.  No legal violations
      F.  Financial statements

## ONE SELLER'S STORY: Dura-Box Company

"Earn-out" was a new word for Dura-Box owner Raul Fernandez. He appreciated the concept after learning it added 30 percent to his purchase price.

Fernandez was a reluctant seller when first approached by his main supplier, Packaging Corporation of America, a subsidiary of Tenneco, Inc. He had devoted twelve years to his Albuquerque, New Mexico, packaging manufacturing business, leading it from ground zero to $2 million annual sales.

The notion of selling made him uneasy. What if he traded the family business for too little? "I wasn't ready to sell," he says. "I got a little nervous thinking, I've worked so hard and put in a tremendous number of hours—who can pay for that? You wonder what kind of price someone can put on your business that makes you happy. You have to get a number that you can live with for the rest of your life. But I knew that sooner or later it would happen. The little guy in the paper business, especially a small manufacturing plant like mine, is bound to be eaten up by the big guy."

When Fernandez started in 1975 Packaging Corporation executives joked that as soon as he reached a certain size, they would be looking to buy him out. Fernandez knew they were serious years later when company vice presidents arrived on the corporate jet from Evanston, Illinois, to tour his facilities. Soon afterward he received a letter of intent. Packaging Corp wanted to buy Dura-Box stock for $500,000 payable in installments over three years.

Torn by fears of selling too low, yet knowing a sale was inevitable, Fernandez stalled for the next two years. His reluctance was emotional. Even before the offer he conferred with his accountant and studied pretax earnings on assets (they were earning 16 to 20 percent). The accountant concurred the business was worth $500,000. Nevertheless, Fernandez held out, meeting and talking with Packaging Corporation, even allowing its accountants access to his records for due diligence, but signing nothing.

Fernandez describes his eventual capitulation: "I saw the way Packaging Corporation was gearing up and wanted to be part of it. If I was going to sell to someone I was going to sell to that company. I used to receive letter after letter from other buyers, but they were smaller and it didn't make much sense to merge or go with someone who didn't have the strength."

Though tiny compared with the buyer's parent company, he wasn't afraid of being consumed by a massive corporation. He even liked the idea. "Being bought by a large company helped make up my mind. I knew I wasn't going to work for a fly-by-night operation. They're going to be here for years."

While both sides agreed at the outset that Fernandez would continue to manage Dura-Box, he didn't know how the earn-out altered his purchase price and working arrangement until negotiations. Packaging Corporation offered a three-year earn-out based on Dura-Box pretax profits. In Year One Fernandez receives 50 percent of all profits over $70,000, in Year Two he receives 50 percent of profits over $80,000, and in Year Three 50 percent over $90,000. The maximum he takes out is $150,000.

Though Fernandez preferred the cash, he saw the earn-out's appeal: "I would have taken the $650,000 and run. But they wanted to keep me, which makes sense. So I go to work with a little incentive."

Fernandez and the buyer negotiated through the mail. At least three times he returned the agreement to the buyer with counter-proposals. The sticking points were the profit percentages in the earn-out and the length of his employment contract. The buyer originally offered to divvy up profits over three years 60–40, 50–50 and 40–60 percent. They settled at 50–50 for all three years. Fernandez wanted a five-year employment contract; he ended up with three and a possibility of renewal. He assumed the title of general manager reporting to a Packaging Corporation vice president.

They made a special arrangement for accounts receivable: if any accounts were still due after a year they became Fernandez's responsibility and expense. Fernandez also indemnified the buyer for potential liabilities. He explains: "With some liabilities you just don't know what's going to happen. Like employee lawsuits. Somebody gets hurt that you don't know about before the acquisition and this guy sues Packaging Corporation. That would create a terrible hassle."

There was no disagreement over the noncompete clause: Fernandez would not engage in the packaging business for one year anywhere in New Mexico or other states where Dura-Box had clients. Unfortunately for Fernandez, they did not bargain over the terms of his installment payments—his notes did not pay interest.

The final version of the purchase agreement was thirty-two pages long, and they signed and closed on the same day. Everyone met in an office in Albuquerque where for two hours Fernandez and his wife unceremoniously signed papers. Though Fernandez had a difficult time making up his mind about the sale, his doubts had vanished. "Once you sign that paper," he says, "you can think of millions of things you should have done differently. But you've put down your John Henry so you forget about it. Once you become part of another company you must try to do better to prove to yourself you can do it and prove to them you can do it."

When the formalities concluded Fernandez pocketed his check, returned to work and informed his employees about their new owner.

## MAKING REPRESENTATIONS AND WARRANTIES

Here's the fulcrum of the seesaw—where buyer and seller identify and limit their risks by asking the other side to make certain assurances. **Representations and warranties** are statements of fact and assurances about a company. They are declarations about a company's condition, the quality of information, and future liabilities and the seller's promise to stand behind them.

A seller's reps and warrants are essential to a buyer. A seller will have to assert that specific documents, legal agreements, company conditions and other facts are accurate and true. A seller may have to rep and warrant financial statements and tax returns, asserting they accurately reflect the company's financial condition and known taxes. This assurance may extend to past or reworked statements. A seller should be cautious of giving assurances about future changes in a company's financial condition and avoid "forward-looking" representations. No one wants to be held to predictions.

A seller may rep and warrant the status of assets, confirming legal, marketable title, full authority to sell them and the absence of any liens or other encumbrances. A buyer especially wants these assurances for intangible assets such as patents, trademarks and copyrights. If a business has numerous contracts and licenses a seller guarantees they are valid and transferable.

In short, a seller declares that nothing has been hidden or misrepresented or is contrary to what a buyer has been told. A seller should be cautious about making general disclosure reps and warrants. While a buyer wants blanket, absolute guarantees, a seller cannot know everything. So in many statements a seller interjects such qualifications as, "To the best of my knowledge. . . ."

The most important reps and warranties cover liabilities—

known, unknown and contingent. Here a seller is asked to reveal conditions or potential conditions that could have financial consequences for the new owner. These are gingerly negotiated between the buyer and seller. Both sides want to limit financial responsibility for known and unknown future events and answer the question, "Who picks up the problems and risks we don't know about?"

In the area of known liabilities a buyer asks for details on litigation, government actions, potential tax liabilities, or compliance with state or federal laws. While not trying to hide anything, a seller may want to reveal only actions that could have a *material* effect on the company, believing that a long list of puny actions would be difficult to compile. A buyer may argue for details about every action so as to judge all possible impacts. Lawyers usually get in a great tug-of-war over this issue of comprehensive information versus relevant information (in legalese, the **materiality** question).

A buyer's reps and warrants are fewer, particularly in an asset sale. While a buyer worries about all sorts of "What ifs?" and hidden liabilities, a seller's concerns usually surround payment and promises about employees or the operation of a company. A buyer asserts his company is legally empowered to complete the sale and make legally binding contracts.

In a sale with notes or stock a buyer reps and warrants the company's financial condition, its ability to meet obligations, that the paper is authorized, valid and transferable, and that stock is registered or unregistered. A buyer may rep and warrant to honor employment contracts, union contracts, severance agreements, pension plans or bonus arrangements. If a buyer is a subsidiary a seller may ask for reps and warrants from the parent company.

Reps and warrants are valid and true (or "survive," as lawyers say) for specific periods of time. Once they have expired, the other party cannot make financial claims. Various reps and warrants are usually tiered—that is, they have different expiration dates. The validity of financial or tax assertions may last until the next audit, lawsuits may be assigned a fixed number of years, and environmental liabilities may survive indefinitely. This is another area where lawyers are often at loggerheads.

## BACKING PROMISES WITH DOLLARS: INDEMNIFICATION

Representations and warranties are really only half of the equation. **Indemnification** spells out what happens if the promises and facts turn out to be untrue or somehow change.

A seller indemnifies a buyer by promising to reimburse losses arising from unknown liabilities, claims, false information or misrepresentations. Indemnification is insurance against the breach of reps and warranties. Negotiating the maximum amount of indemnification captures everyone's attention.

A seller indemnifies a buyer against individual contingencies or a collection of possible liabilities. Separate indemnifications may be for tax liabilities, unsettled lawsuits or claims by individuals. What a seller indemnifies and for how much depends on the circumstances of the company, the buyer's assessment of potential cost, and striking a bargain.

An indemnification can be a single amount for all contingencies or separate amounts for individual claims. Negotiators call the maximum amount a seller guarantees a **ceiling**. A seller has no responsibility for claims or damages over and above this. Frequently sellers bargain for an amount that represents a minimum amount a seller will guarantee against an assortment of claims. Called a **basket**, it lumps together many individual indemnifications. A buyer agrees not to make any claims against the seller for less than the value of the basket. If a basket is $100,000 a buyer cannot ask for payment for claims for less. A basket eliminates lots of little claims.

But if the total amount of claims exceeds the basket, the seller pays. This raises another issue. The two parties have to negotiate whether the seller is responsible only for claims over the basket or for the basket amount plus everything above it. Does a seller's responsibility begin at $100,000 or at zero but isn't payable unless the amount reaches $100,000?

Indemnification varies tremendously from sale to sale and company to company. It may represent a small fraction of the purchase price, such as 5 percent, or the entire purchase price. Many negotiators insist that sellers indemnify the buyer up to the total purchase price. To collect on a violation of a representation or warrant, buyers make a claim against the seller. Occasionally, a buyer insists that part of the purchase price be deposited into a special **escrow account** to pay for possible claims and remain there until the indemnification period expires.

A seller wants indemnification to be in force for as little time as possible. Normally indemnification lasts as long as the relevant rep and warrant. Escrow deposits typically survive from one to five years. Some potential liabilities may linger for years. On a possible environmental cleanup action, a seller may have to indemnify a buyer forever.

Occasionally tables are turned and a buyer indemnifies a seller. If a buyer pays with stock or notes a seller can ask for collateral (a mortgage or company assets, for instance) to ensure payment. In a sale involving outside, third-party financing, a buyer may indemnify a seller against claims from the source of financing.

## CLOSING MECHANICS

> "At closing there were no problems but a circus of people. Two would be talking to each other and another three would be off in a corner trying to figure something else out. And I'm making the rounds saying, 'What's your problem?' and 'Oh, he has that information on the table over there' and 'We signed that last week.' "   —Ken Rothman

Signing the agreement is not closing—it's agreeing to its terms. Closing is the actual transfer of a company—handing over title to assets or stock certificates and accepting a check, certificates or proof the money has been deposited into the seller's account. Some people call closing "passing," implying the passing on of documents and property.

Closing is either simultaneous with signing or later. It's usually separate if people are awaiting government antitrust approval, tax rulings or an opinion from the Securities and Exchange Commission about stock registration. Both parties may have to produce documents or perform certain tasks before closing. Sometimes a buyer must obtain a written authorization for a sale from the board of directors.

Given a choice, simultaneous closing is preferable. Signing and closing on the same day eliminates the uncertain time when a company has a binding contract but is awaiting transfer, a time when unforeseen events can mar or endanger a sale. A single event also simplifies the purchase agreement because a seller does not have to make promises about the conduct of the business between signing and closing.

Closing is scheduled for a day and time, usually in the offices of either side's lawyer. A seller should push for the earliest possible closing date. Time is money, and every day a company is in limbo means one less day an owner has either a company or money. If the purchase price is fixed and the sale not closed by a certain date, a seller can ask for interest on the money until closing.

## ONE SELLER'S STORY: Spencer Foods, Inc.

Spencer Foods was an attractive yet troubled company. Although the country's third largest beef packer with revenues around $500 million, it was marginally profitable with erratic earnings. When Bud Pearson decided to sell he faced the challenge of carving out the best possible deal under adverse pressures. He wasn't going to give it away, but he was well aware of its shortcomings. He found the solution in a complex agreement that gave him and his fellow shareholders their price and the buyer the protections and assurances it demanded.

Tucked into the flatlands of northwest Iowa, Spencer Foods was a large beef-packing company controlled and managed by chairman, CEO and president Bud Pearson. It possessed rich assets and, not incidentally, large potential liabilities and bad labor relations at its plant in Spencer. The assets attracted a steady stream of would-be buyers; the liabilities, inconsistent earnings and losing lines of business cooled their ardor.

Spencer Foods bought cattle from all over the country, butchered the meat, then sold the carcasses to retailers and wholesalers.

While a staple in the meat industry for decades, the business came into vogue in the late 1960s. Prices were high and meat companies were prized. Spencer Foods went public in 1965, selling about 40 percent of its stock, and charming investors. Within a few years shares were selling for twenty-five times earnings, a high-priced testimony to their popularity.

Around the same time Bud Pearson expanded. He recounts, "In the late sixties we decided we wanted to diversify, become more than just a meat packer: 'Let's become a food company.' We were trying to get a little pizazz into our stock. So we acquired a plant in Florida with branded products." The company also purchased leather-tanning plants in Massachusetts and Milwaukee.

Not surprisingly, buyers swarmed around Spencer Foods like flies. Armour Company came courting as did Green Giant Company, but neither reached the altar. Nevertheless, these buyers whetted shareholders' appetites. "They got all the major shareholders thinking about selling," Pearson says. "They had a smell of it." Quickening their appetites was the change in fortune in the beef-packing business. "We went out of vogue as quickly as we went in," he recalls. Costly union contracts added to their troubles.

Pearson remembers: "It seemed that every three years when our contracts expired we went on strike. Our big cash cow was in Schuyler, Nebraska. Then we would take a strike at the Spencer plant and it would wipe out our profits. There were just too many problems. That was probably one of the major reasons we were amenable to selling, because the labor problems at Spencer seemed insurmountable. It was very difficult to open up a plant with non-union labor. It was something we didn't have the appetite for, and it would have been a bloody mess. We were at the mercy of the union and we knew it. But we knew a new owner could come in and open up the plant."

Spencer Foods went looking for a buyer. The search was conducted by a board member who was a lawyer and experienced deal maker. Concentrating on the agricultural industry and the Midwest, he discovered Land O' Lakes, a Minneapolis co-op. Pearson liked what he learned about the company. "It was a strong co-op. We knew they were the largest feed company in Iowa, and we knew they were successful. And we did some checking into their net worth. [They have annual reports they send out to members, and some of that stuff was in there.] There was no doubt about their financial fortitude."

The two parties met at a lawyer's office in Omaha. Six people attended, including both presidents and their attorneys. They were friendly, attentive and just a touch cautious. Because Spencer Foods was publicly held, Land O' Lakes had access to reams of information. "They had our 10-K and they knew a lot about us, so that definitely shortened the introductory part," Pearson says. To further entice the buyer, Pearson brought along asset appraisals for the company's major facilities.

Price was not openly discussed, but Pearson was sensitive to how the stock market valued Spencer Foods. "Our P/E on continuing operations had slipped to five, but we weren't interested in selling at that kind of price. We had in our minds that we ought to bring at least book value." Book value [the net value of assets determined by the balance sheet amount of outstanding capital stock and retained earnings] was $13 million.

Pearson recalls Land O' Lakes' proposal: "They let us know right at the outset that their basic interest was in the Spencer operation and the operation in Nebraska. These were in their area. They were interested just in the basic beef business. They wanted us to sell off the other facilities. And they wanted to make a cash acquisition for the facilities—they wanted an asset purchase." The proposal made sense. By purchasing select assets, Land O' Lakes would not assume union contracts or unprofitable properties.

"We said that might work out," Pearson remembers. "But we needed to research how it would affect the shareholders and the tax implications." The meeting ended with Land O' Lakes arranging to tour the Spencer plant and Pearson promising to provide additional financial information and appraisals.

The next meeting, weeks later, produced more documents and numbers and a willingness to begin formal negotiations. To accommodate all the participants and to maintain secrecy ["We tried to keep it quiet at first. It can be a little upsetting to your people so you try not to do it under their noses," Pearson says.], negotiators gathered in different Midwest cities. The buyer had a large team: in-house counsel, outside counsel including the senior partner of a national law firm, finance executives, three vice presidents and the president. "Good strategy on their part," Pearson reflects. On the Spencer side was Pearson, the executive vice president, a finance executive, a lawyer and an outside director.

The Spencer people were firm in asking for book value. But with negative earnings, the $13 million figure appeared shaky. So they worked out a compromise. Land O' Lakes would pay book value for assets as long as net worth did not slip below $11.5 million by the end of the fiscal year. Below that figure, Spencer would have to make up the price.

On some points, management contracts was one, Pearson and his buyers were in complete accord. "I knew there was no way they would buy the operation and put in their own management," Pearson remembers. "There was no way. That was stated at the outset: 'We don't know how to run a meat-packing operation, and we want management to continue. Management is crucial.' "

A discovery by the Spencer camp changed the entire direction of negotiations. The tax experts concluded that an asset sale would be very costly to Pearson and his fellow owners. An asset sale was out of the picture, he told the Minneapolis co-op. For the buyer, purchasing stock instead of assets was rife with peril. The buyer could not pick and choose safe properties or exclude certain contracts and liabilities from the deal. Buying Spencer Foods stock meant acquiring the entire company—assets, liabilities, and hidden, off-balance sheet conditions—unless the purchase agreement contained protections.

Now came the hard part for Pearson and his fellow negotiators: satisfying the buyer's worries without making concessions that would haunt and cost them later.

The buyer still wanted only the Iowa and Nebraska beef-processing facilities. To configure the company Land O' Lakes wanted, Pearson agreed to sell the other assets prior to the sale. If they couldn't sell them Pearson and insider shareholders agreed to buy the properties themselves. In the end they had to purchase two of the facilities.

Other conditions had to be met. Pearson explains: "One thing that stymied us was an antitrust action by a group of cattle feeders. With that action hanging over us, Land O' Lakes was not anxious to close. To make this acquisition, they said, 'You're going to have to get that lawsuit out of the way.' " An outstanding lawsuit can be handled in one of two ways. An agreement can assign responsibility for its outcome or, as with Spencer Foods, the buyer may insist that it's cleared up before the sale.

"Being a farmers' group," Pearson says, "Land O' Lakes wasn't interested in buying this kind of lawsuit. And we weren't interested in indemnifying them, either. They had some clout with the people suing, and they were instrumental in getting it cleared up. The suit was for several million dollars, and we settled for $425,000."

When the sale became a stock purchase the warranties assumed enormous importance. They became the nucleus of the agreement. "We had to warrant many different things. It was pages long, and the warranties probably went beyond what you would normally do. They didn't want any surprises," Pearson reports. Major shareholders who were directors had to warrant the company's net worth and accounting procedures. They had to guarantee that the balance sheet showed all liabilities or reserves for liabilities *known and unknown* for events up to closing day.

Indemnification normally goes hand in hand with warranties. One way the seller backs guarantees is with an escrow deposit to pay for claims by a buyer. Given the extensive warranties in this sale, the buyer could have demanded indemnification up to the entire purchase price. But no seller wants to stake everything on the warranties.

Instead of wrestling over the amount of indemnification, buyer and seller found a compromise: an installment sale for the major stockholders and cash for the public stockholders. Land O' Lakes paid the purchase price over three years in increments of 10 percent, 45 percent and the balance (less $1 million for warranties) a year later. The notes paid 8 percent interest. Pearson was pleased. "It gave them some protection if something came up. They still had the money to hold back. It was good for us because we got to spread taxable income over a number of years."

Worries about warranties and unexpected losses or claims continued to nag both buyer and seller. More guarantees were written into the agreement. Pearson's employment agreement enabled him to create a cushion against future claims. He explains: "Part of the agreement was that we [major stockholders] could build up a reserve against any contingencies. A certain percent of the earnings would go toward any contingencies for the next three years. Anything that might come up from the original warranties. If something that we would be liable for worth say $1 million came out of the woodwork, we would be covered by any excess earnings over $6.25 million a year."

As astute sellers Pearson and his associates carefully defined how to calculate earnings. "We laid that out. We designated what the corporate charges could be, and interest was thrown out. Earnings were pretax, pre-interest." He says that after the sale the formula became more complicated, but allowances had been made. "It looked fairly simple at first, but it got more complex. We made some acquisitions that complicated it down the line. So we negotiated again."

The definition of earnings was important to Pearson for another reason. His three-year contract paid him 25 percent of Spencer Foods earnings over a certain mark. Other conditions of the agreement were a noncompete for five years and the title of president of the new Land O' Lakes subsidiary. One element of the agreement he didn't worry about was termination. "That was not a threat. I knew they needed me. The continuation of management was important to them. They were well aware that in this industry those who succeed are those who have been in it a long time and have the expertise."

Negotiations lasted almost a year. The deal grew increasingly complex as the buyer organized a separate company to finance the purchase, notified the Securities and Exchange Commission and tendered its offer to the public shareholders, who held about half of Spencer Foods stock.

Behind the scenes Pearson found the process tiring and trying. "It took so much time because the Land O' Lakes financing effort took six months. It tested your patience, especially when they had people chipping away at you. You had to bite your tongue occasionally. Though tempers sometimes got short it was amicable. Good chemistry was important because if they saw it wasn't there, there would be no deal. They were depending on me to stay on and run it. They knew that and I knew that. And it wouldn't happen if we didn't get along."

For signing and closing, the entire Spencer Foods board of directors traveled to Minneapolis. Stock certificates had been delivered earlier and checks were mailed afterward. All that was required was signatures. Signing took place at a hotel. It was crisp and businesslike. The Spencer Foods people saved celebrating for later when they all gathered for drinks, dinner and congratulations.

## MAKING PLANS: EMPLOYMENT CONTRACTS AND NONCOMPETES

"The employment contract made sense to me. I felt comfortable with it. There were promises I had to make, but there were promises they made to me. Things like if my salary were to be reduced, then it was because everybody's salary had to be reduced. Guarantees that if there were a layoff I would have time to find another job."

—Tim Bachman

Most buyers seek continuity and want the people who made a company profitable to keep running it, albeit under new leadership. Two or three years is a common contract period. It reassures a buyer of a reasonable commitment and gives a seller time to generate bonus-producing earnings. Generally after three years, both sides reassess their relationship and decide whether the marriage works.

A workable **employment contract** anticipates situations, good and bad, and raises "What ifs?" Imagining the up side is easy: seller and buyer like the arrangement, and the acquired company exceeds its earnings target. A seller's main concern in this instance is sharing in company profits. This concern can be relieved with a performance bonus based on a percentage of earnings, and an added premium if earnings top a certain level.

The thorniest "What if?" surrounds cancellation. What if seller or buyer want out? All employment contracts contain conditions and penalties for termination. Normally, they assume a traditional employer-employee relationship and describe why and how each side can break off. But the relationship between buyer and seller is more complicated than between employer and employee. Subtle, unspoken issues like ego, status and independence come into play. Any of these can push a seller or buyer to cancel an agreement or force the other side to cancel.

A seller must anticipate all kinds of termination: termination without cause or reason, resignation forced by stripping of responsibilities, a mutual parting over a dispute about the financial terms of the contract. Terms have to be defined and agreed upon, particularly "cause" and what constitutes "voluntary" and "involuntary" termination. And a seller has to be mindful of not forfeiting severance pay, bonuses or installment payments in a forced resignation.

An employment contract is a legal document and, in theory, enforceable by law. In practice, it may not be enforceable. A buyer would have a hard time forcing an employee to stay against his will. If a seller leaves and forfeits compensation or severance payments there is little a buyer can do to stop him or her. Equally important to a seller are responsibilities and fitting into the company hierarchy. A seller is cautious about accepting a titular role in the new company, adding continuity to the corporate letterhead but possessing no substantive authority. Title alone does not guarantee a voice in the new entity. The job description specifies to whom the seller reports. The implications of the chain of command are clear: a seller reporting to the chief executive officer has more influence and independence than someone reporting to a subsidiary president or chief operating officer.

A seller with an employment contract is a changed person. Motives and priorities shift. As an owner, a seller labors for compensation other than a paycheck. The motivation and rewards are often intangible: personal satisfaction, the challenge of building a company, independence and freedom to make decisions. As an employee, a seller's incentives are dollars and cents. Buyer and seller should recognize this by enhancing the incentives not only with salary but also a performance bonus. This bonus is essential. It keeps a seller's interest and generates energy. A seller should also make sure that credits toward vesting in a company pension plan are carried over to the new employment contract so that years and money are not lost.

A covenant not to compete is either in the employment contract or, for sellers not staying on, separate. Frequently key executives in the seller's company are also asked to sign a noncompete. A signer agrees not to engage in the same business as the buyer and the acquired company for a certain number of years.

A **noncompete** restrains a seller in three ways: number of years, geography and line of business. All these elements are negotiable and a buyer may pay for noncompetes. The amount varies, depending on the restrictions and other components of the purchase price. A noncompete covenant is taxable income to a seller and deductible by a buyer if the amount is reasonable. If a buyer does not put a price on it the IRS can claim it is goodwill. For this reason, a buyer puts some value on the noncompete covenant. The amount may be substantial or, if a seller is satisfied with the overall purchase price, a token amount.

A buyer usually wants a noncompete in effect as long as possible, and a seller usually wants the shortest term. The meeting ground is usually somewhere between two and four years.

Compromise may also be needed on the geographical area covered by a noncompete. The seller of a company with a national or international market may not compete anywhere. A seller of a regional firm or a company doing business in one city may be limited to that part of the country. Some noncompetes break the area down to miles, as for service or retail businesses.

The noncompete states what business the seller must avoid. A seller wants the narrowest definition possible, for freedom to pursue similar if not directly competitive lines of work. To narrow the noncompete, a seller describes forbidden products, goods, services or processes. A variation is to name customers or clients a seller is prohibited from doing business with.

A final point in the noncompete may be a **nonraiding clause** —a seller's pledge not to recruit former employees from the buyer's company. As with other restrictions in the noncompete, this should be circumscribed within a number of years. For a seller, the fewer the better. You want to limit your options and possibilities as little as possible.

## PROTECTING EMPLOYEES

If a buyer purchases assets, the status of employees and their benefits may be up for grabs. A buyer is not necessarily bound by the agreements of the former owner. For the buyer of stock, the employee question may be reduced to policies: Does the new owner continue where the seller left off with the same arrangements for salaries, severance, pensions and other benefits? Sellers concerned about employees have to negotiate over which benefits continue after the sale.

Collective bargaining agreements are delicate. Change of ownership, especially in an asset sale, can trigger great deliberations over whether and which labor contracts and other employee commitments survive.

Unexercised employee stock options must be provided for. Depending on their terms, they can be exercised before a sale or later. Sometimes employees are paid cash for the difference between the option price and sale price. If the company is public, a buyer may substitute its stock for the seller's. Like severance pay, stock options represent money. Their value has to be calculated and recognized. A buyer interested in fairness to employees will allow them to exercise options within a thirty- to ninety-day period.

Severance pay can be tricky if a selling company has a policy based on accumulated years with a company. A policy that pays a week's salary for every year served represents a substantial obligation in a company with many employees working for many years. Buyer and seller must decide who assumes it after the sale. One solution is to split the obligation. For employees who leave a company within six months (or a year), a seller pays their severance. For employees who stay longer than six months or a year and whom presumably the buyer wants to keep, the buyer pays severance.


## MISCELLANEOUS AND ESSENTIAL EXTRAS

Expenses connected with a sale—for auditors, attorneys, finders, appraisers—can be designated the responsibility of one party. Usually each party pays its own costs but some expenses fall to neither.

A common point of contention is who pays the transfer tax, a sales tax imposed by some states when assets are sold. In a stock exchange, expenses for legal fees and transferring ownership have to be negotiated, particularly when a seller receives no cash.

For personal property, side deals are often arranged between seller and buyer. A common side deal is for a seller to keep personal office furnishings, the company car, or company documents or memos. A letter from the buyer to the seller outlining their understanding is usually sufficient. Side letters can also be written to stipulate last-minute delivery of timely, sensitive information, such as trade secrets. The purchase agreement should reference these side letters.

Lots of documents are attached to the purchase agreement. Without them, clauses may be meaningless or unenforceable. They substantiate representations and warranties. Many exhibits are lists of papers a seller collects. Here are some exhibits and disclosure statements that may be attached to your agreement:

- Description of all real estate property
- Description of assets, inventory and products
- Description schedules for office furniture and equipment
- Copies of leases, contracts, accounts, loan agreements, credit lines
- Names of suppliers, customers, clients and the dollar value of their business
- Names of employees under contract and their compensation
- Copies of insurance policies
- Details of litigation or pending tax audits
- Shareholders' power of attorney giving majority shareholder authority to enter into this agreement and sign for other shareholders
- Notices filed with government offices regarding business activities (e.g., environmental permits) and execution of the sale (e.g., notification of acquisition required by the Hart-Scott-Rodino Act)
- Accounting formulas, principles and definitions used in calculating an earn-out or installment sale

- Escrow agreements
- Financial statements, copies of stock certificates

## CLOSING IN

For a seller who has signed the purchase agreement but not closed, it's limbo time. On the surface, nothing looks different. Your company is operating as usual. You still make decisions and worry about production schedules, cash flow and marketing designs. But underneath, it's different. There's nothing left to negotiate. Soon you will be either gone or reporting to someone else. A new owner will buy your worries.

This is no time to let down your guard. Your company has to be guided closely so nothing interferes with the terms of your agreement. A seller should assume the role of a diligent caretaker who is keeping the promises about operating the business between signing and closing. Talk to the buyer regularly about operations. In the language of agreements, "Conduct the business and affairs of the company only in the usual and ordinary course."

This means a seller can't make extraordinary expenditures or commitments (sometimes this is defined as anything over a certain amount), hire or fire without cause or reason, change salaries or the normal compensation policy, cancel accounts, contracts or lines of credit, or alter normal accounting practices. In short, a seller can't do anything to change a company's financial condition or reputation with outsiders.

Any number of events or developments could jeopardize a sale, so a seller scrupulously guards the company. A natural disaster or accident—flood, fire or casualty—may nullify a seller's representations and warranties. Legal action, such as a product liability suit, indictment of employees for drug dealing, or challenges by minority shareholders or former business associates, can delay or kill a sale. A seller's best strategy for keeping a company intact is to move quickly to closing day.

To close, buyers and sellers often gather at the offices of the buyer's attorney. Friday seems to be a popular closing day. A seller who is majority shareholder or has power of attorney to sign for other shareholders may come alone. If stock certificates have not been transferred the seller delivers them. Sellers should ask their attorney to accompany them to make sure all documents are in order and in case of a last-minute question or alteration. A buyer usually has lots of people at closing—signers, attorneys and accountants for all interested parties. If a buyer is financing a sale or loans are being paid off and liens released, bank representatives may participate.

There's little preparation for closing. A seller's job is to sign papers, a task that may stretch for hours and cover hundreds of pages. A seller should be ready to do something with the money. A smart seller arranges a safe interest-bearing place to park it, as in a certificate of deposit or Treasury bill, or arranges with a money manager to invest it immediately. Sale money should not sit around in a checking account.

Closing may take hours or, if terms are unsettled, days. Surprisingly, many sellers say there's little ceremony or celebration. It's a business event, albeit once-in-a-lifetime for some, but still commonplace. More often than not, a seller finishes closing and returns to the office to clear out or keep working. What you've done takes more than a day to sink in.

# AFTERMATH

> "We have a wonderful relationship. He [the buyer] has no interest at all in my business. He doesn't stick his nose in the business. He doesn't care about the business. He wants to know that I'm happy and he wants to see my bottom line. As long as I can continue doing that, producing that bottom line, we have an excellent relationship. It's been six months now and I'm not operating any differently than a year ago. Except I'm a public company."
> —Steve Rosendorf

## GOODBYE ENTREPRENEUR—HELLO EMPLOYEE

The deed is done. Your baby, your creation, the business you devoted years to nurturing and growing now belongs to someone else. In spirit, you've relinquished the corner office, employees call another person "Boss," and a new name appears on corporate checks. These changes sound superficial, and in a way they are. But they also indicate a fundamental shift that for many sellers requires their biggest adjustment.

Immediately after a sale, the majority of sellers stay with their old company and work with the new owner. Their reasons are many: Money. Lack of another job. An attachment to the company and a desire to be part of its next phase of growth. Ambition to be a major player in the buyer's company. To ensure earn-outs produce. Some sellers are pleased and find the new environment invigorating. Free of the worries and pressures of ownership and bolstered by the support of a robust parent company, they relish making their former business even more profitable.

The transition from entrepreneur, owner and seller to recruit, employee and wage earner is arduous. Your role has changed and your company is about to change. A seller joins an unfamiliar employment world with new people, new ways of doing things and new attitudes. The buyer's world does not change for the newcomer; the newcomer adapts. It can be done and be immensely rewarding. Sellers who successfully join the buyer's organization contribute to building a bigger, more prosperous company while increasing their personal wealth.

The buyer's company is probably larger, more rigid and more methodical. The former entrepreneur will encounter more committees, memorandums and demands for quarterly results. A seller now interacts with another layer of executives and attends more meetings: sales meetings, planning meetings, shareholder meetings, executive retreats. The meeting becomes a primary communication channel. With more meetings comes more travel—regular trips to the head office or somewhere in-between.

An acquired company can become an independent operating company or a subsidiary. This gives the seller's company a degree of independence. The two companies may also be physically distant, adding to a seller's autonomy. For sellers uncomfortable with supervision or authority, the farther away the better. Given a company with a separate business structure and which is more or less self-contained, a buyer's overseeing depends on how well the acquisition functions and what it contributes to other operating units and/or the parent.

Sellers to publicly held buyers have more reporting requirements and expenses. Public companies report quarterly results to shareholders and the SEC. To assemble these figures, buyers constantly push their acquisitions to provide operating results. For the seller's company, these reporting requirements bring more deadlines and expenses. Personnel must be hired to prepare financial reports and forecasts and to institute accounting systems.

The seller also has to pick up a share of overhead costs from the parent company to cover expenses for the new acquisition.

Working with the new owner brings surprises. Sellers may discover their expectations and assumptions about the marriage to be part fantasy. They may be unprepared for the dramatic change a sale brings, particularly if a buyer promised the company would operate as before. If a seller thought through the sale process, the obvious realization would be "Of course the buyer is going to change my company. If I were the buyer I'd change it, too." But sellers sometimes don't think beyond getting their money. Subtle at first, changes are inevitable.

Personally, sellers redefine their self-image. While the label "entrepreneur" has been overworked and appropriated by the likes of gourmet popcorn vendors, it still means something to the individual who built a viable commercial venture. One's identity is wrapped up in what one does, and a seller is no longer an entrepreneur—he or she is an employee. Admitting and accepting it can shake your confidence and opinion of yourself. For many sellers, the only consolation is that it won't last long. Either they rise to the top of the new company or their employment ends.

An early realization is that the seller is no longer the boss. Final authority to make decisions, commit substantial amounts of money, hire and fire managers—to be responsible for how a company performs—has disappeared. The company has a new hierarchy. A seller reports to someone else. Whether it's a vice president or the chairman, a seller has lost the freedom to execute ideas and commit resources independently. Things must be cleared and approved.

The loss of this control can be discomforting. Control and the appeal of leadership is why people go into their own business; they like directing and managing and being a general. For natural leaders, following does not come easily.

Meshing with the new company demands adjustments by employees as well as sellers. Except in very large sales, the acquisition will probably be supervised by the buyer's middle management. These people are responsible for fitting together the pieces of the seller's and buyer's companies. The acquisition is their new turf and the seller's people, their fresh troops.

The middle managers of the two companies may clash as they battle for authority and their way of doing things. The seller's managers resist or acquiesce, depending on the nature of the skirmish. But despite feelings about prior understandings on doing things differently, the seller's employees usually do most of the bending and compromising.

A seller may encounter another reaction from middle managers. It is a "we-they" attitude that relegates a seller to the ranks of outsider with little influence in the company. A seller is joining an institution where cliques and loyalties are already established. An alert seller, aware of the potential problem, avoids the outsider stigma by becoming part of the buyer's crowd. Instead of being aloof and separate, a seller participates in activities, social events and company gatherings, and finds a niche among the buyer's ranks.

Employees of the former owner may feel uneasy. They're more vulnerable and must prove their worth to the new boss. Veteran employees may feel abandoned and cut off. Years of service and loyalty to the former owner often mean little to the buyer. The sale has cleaned their slate. Although they may not have lost accrued benefits, they may have lost status and incentives. Their career path has been cut short by the new owner. Providing incentives for remaining employees in acquired firms is a special problem. Sellers concerned about their employees have to impress upon the buyer the importance of keeping motivated, loyal employees.

Buyers are not stupid. They know they need productive employees to make an acquisition succeed. They are doing something of a juggling act—evaluating remaining employees to see if they fit the new scheme and simultaneously trying to win their loyalty and labors.

For some, the buyer presents opportunity—a bigger pond with bigger fish. A manager or vice president in the seller's company may have had nowhere to advance—the next rung up was the owner's job. In the buyer's company a vice president may have all sizes of mountains to conquer—divisions, subsidiaries, corporate headquarters.

Cooperation and compromise are probably more valued than originality and the ability to think and react quickly. The surviving seller understands that promises and plans made during negotiations may not materialize, especially if they are not in the purchase agreement. Conversations with the buyer about expansion, shifted emphasis, and more resources may be quickly forgotten. A seller has to assume a buyer is going to remodel the company. The question is, "How much?" These changes may not match the original scenario and may be counter to what the former owner thinks best. But they're no longer a seller's worries.

Differing expectations may lead to conflicts. A seller waits for the new owner to inject new capital or hire more workers while a buyer waits for the seller to cut expenses and prepare three-year profit-and-loss projections. A seller's employment contract defines some responsibilities and expectations, but no agreement covers everything. Gray areas surface as buyer and seller carry out their jobs and test the arrangement. Only a shared vision sees them through and makes the new partnership last.

## CUTTING LOOSE—RULES TO SELL BY

> "The stated reason most sellers leave their business may be, 'By God, I'm an entrepreneur and I want to do it myself.' But we're not as adaptable in a corporate sense as we sometimes think. Somebody buys you, they buy you. They have the right to run you, and they think they run you better than you do."
> —Bill King

Most sellers leave an acquired company within five years of a sale. Whether by choice or force, former owners exhibit a poor track record for staying in the corporate fold. (And buyers exhibit an even more dismal record for making acquisitions work, but that's another book.) Entrepreneurism and independent streaks run deep. Regardless of the financial incentives and the lure of security, sellers itch to be their own masters once more. Restlessness may be fueled by the flush of success. They think, I cashed in once—maybe I can do it again. A few retire or recharge their batteries while trying to figure out what next. But some test the idea of another venture and take the first tentative steps.

If you are leaning in that direction these Rules to Sell By are

reminders or guideposts for the evolution and successful sale of
your second company.

## #1. WELL-STRUCTURED, WELL-SOLD

The well-managed company created for a prosperous, independent
life sells better than the company with thin, careless management
and shaky finances. This rule isn't as self-evident as it sounds. The
well-structured company pays less attention to sale prospects than
to management and finances. By paying more attention to internal
operations than to selling, the well-structured company becomes a
hot sale target. Ironically, the company with an eager eye on selling
and designed for a quick liquidation doesn't attract the attention
that the company built on solid operating principles and farsighted
management does.

Structure encompasses many facets of a company. It's capable,
young personnel led by experienced executives. It's secure financing
and manageable debt, a strong market position and a long-term
plan. It's organizational pieces such as proper accounting and
bookkeeping, financial controls, incentives to motivate employees,
a useful board of directors or group of advisors.

Another feature is a managerial hierarchy that disperses responsibility. It's one or two vice presidents sharing authority with
the seller/owner. The well-structured firm does not depend on one
personality. The company is greater and stronger than a single
individual.

A corollary to sharing control is creating durable relation-
ships. A seller establishes a strong relationship with a bank through
a dependable performance on commitments and payments, keeping
in regular contact (not just when money is needed) and avoiding
surprises and unexpected troubles. Smart business owners keep
bankers informed of their companies' ups and downs.

They also enlist the services of an attorney familiar with their
line of business, whether it be contracts or international commerce.
An established relationship with a lawyer gives a seller someone to
call on for prompt answers to legal questions. Lawyers are also a
good source of information about local activities—who is incor-

porating, who's going into bankruptcy and who's expanding. This information can be useful to a business owner.

An outside accountant provides a business owner with tax planning and establishes a system of financial controls within a company. This person offers a valuable perspective on a company's financial systems. A professional, independent opinion of a company's financial condition carries a lot of weight with business associates and buyers.

"Well-structured" reaches below the surface. It's a company philosophy that avoids a leverage mentality and burdensome debts and expenses. No business can or wants to work as a cash-and-carry operation. Properly structured debt and skillfully used leverage help a company grow. But with a tight fist on debt and expenses, an owner builds up equity and liquidity.

Strong financial reporting is essential in the well-structured company. The owner arranges for either an annual audit or, in the case of a small company, unaudited statements prepared by an outside accountant. An audit by an independent certified public accountant lends credibility to financial statements, verifies internal accounting controls, and demonstrates that management is sophisticated and scrupulous.

Yes, audits are costly. A young struggling company will certainly balk at the expense. And for some very small firms—revenues under $1 million—an audit may not be justifiable. In this case, at least financial statements should be prepared by an outside accountant.

Retaining earnings are an essential source of growth. Many owners are preoccupied with taxes and so prefer to spend profits to reduce their bill with the IRS. Small private businesses are notorious for substantial expenditures for travel and entertainment, expensive office art, club memberships, superfluous personnel, airplanes, boats and even hunting resorts. While they pay lower taxes, their retained earnings and net worth are minuscule. Unnecessary expenses cut into the money a company retains. A company with little retained earnings has no cushion against hard times. It's also less appealing to a buyer because it cannot show its earning capacity.

### #2. THINK THROUGH CONSEQUENCES

Selling a company creates more possibilities than a Chinese menu. Many financial consequences are clear. On the personal level, some sellers immediately apply the proceeds to pay taxes or debts, save for college educations, help relatives. On the professional level, others already have their eye on another business. These are the lucky ones—sellers who know exactly what to do with their new-found wealth.

The bulk of sellers are unprepared for the money. Many have been so preoccupied with running their companies and managing business finances that they have no experience in personal money management. Unable or unwilling to handle personal wealth, they're unaware of investment options and tax implications, or don't know to whom to turn for help. A seller who cashes in has to anticipate myriad financial consequences.

Other consequences take sellers by surprise. Without adequate preparation or anticipation, sellers are besieged by worries about the future, self-doubt, disappointment from unrealistic expectations about the sale itself or the buyer, or hostile reactions from employees or family members. These don't have to happen, not if a seller takes time to map out goals for the sale, pinpoint whom it will affect and how, and anticipate what can happen afterward.

Preparation is everything. A seller who believes that relinquishing ownership of a company has only financial consequences is shortsighted. The simplest way to avoid troubles is to talk over the sale beforehand with family members, other sellers, and the accountant and lawyer. In short, cover all the bases.

### #3. USE OUTSIDE EXPERTS BUT MAKE YOUR OWN BUSINESS DECISIONS

No seller should work alone. Transferring a company to another owner involves too many legal, accounting and tax angles for anyone to execute it solo. Business brokers, investment bankers, accountants, lawyers, appraisers and consultants play a necessary role in a sale. A seller is foolish not to enlist expert advice simply to save a few dollars. The potential loss from inadequate advice could be much greater than any fees.

Paradoxically, these very experts can confuse, delay and even kill a sale. Their attention to detail can bog down a seller in unlikely scenarios or unwarranted fears. Minor points become the focus of attention and contention, and proceedings stalemate. Equally dangerous is when these people slip from areas of expertise and make business decisions for a seller. They get into questions of commerce, marketing, management and money—subjects in which the seller has already demonstrated considerable skill. A seller must insist that experts stick to their well-defined professions and not venture beyond.

#### #4. READ YOUR BUYER THOROUGHLY

Your buyer's motives and thinking are probably more complex and convoluted than yours. For a seller, the deal has a finite end, whether at closing when the price is paid in full or when notes and employment contracts expire. The buyer, however, signs for the long term. Another complication for a buyer is the battalion of other interested parties—shareholders, financial backers, board members, executives and employees—to whom an acquirer must answer. Buyers are often accountable to more people than sellers. All this makes your buyer a very complex person.

Misreading a buyer can ruin a sale. A thorough reading entails knowing why a buyer wants you: Is your company in a glamorous industry and is the buyer chasing a fad? Are your earnings going to fuel the buyer's expansion? Does your company offer a unique distribution system? Do you have patents the buyer covets? The possibilities could fill a notebook. Regardless of which reasons motivate a buyer, ferret them out.

Read how a buyer values and prices a company. Formulas (return on equity, discounted future cash flow, profit before taxes and more) may be applied as well as general principles such as, "We never pay for goodwill" or "Earnings projections are always wrong—let's do an earn-out." Understanding a buyer's methods enables a seller to increase company value.

To read a buyer is to sense fears and worries. Has the buyer been burned on a previous sale or is the buyer under pressure for a certain level of performance or return? Some feature of your company may trigger a negative reaction in a buyer. For example, a buyer may be worried about an environmental lawsuit, key employees leaving or an unexpected market downturn. The insightful seller recognizes a buyer's fears, whether based on emotions or facts, and provides reassurances. A buyer whose fears are recognized and addressed early will usually not back out.

### #5. THE SHAPE OF A SALE IS LIMITED ONLY BY YOUR IMAGINATION

With a willing buyer and a willing seller, a company can be sold a seemingly infinite number of ways. Forget the formulas and yardsticks and principles. These are tools and road signs for reaching your goal. You and the buyer decide what that goal looks like. As long as both sides are willing and flexible, a sale will happen.

The currencies of an acquisition—cash, stock, notes, earnout, installment payments—can be mixed and portioned out in remarkable variety. The same is true for tax concerns. Between the goalposts of "taxable" and "tax-free" lie yards of variations. Portions of the price can be one or the other. Different shareholders can elect for different tax treatments. Buyers can pay a seller's taxes. The options are endless. The two key ingredients are willingness to get the deal done and flexibility.

---

"Selling gave me an opportunity to start over again." —Jim Waters

# GLOSSARY

**appraiser** (aka **business valuation expert**): individual or company specializing in determining the value of a company's assets.

**asset sale:** one of two primary ways (the other is a stock sale) to sell a company. Involves transferring title to select tangible and intangible assets to a buyer.

**asset test ratio:** see quick ratio.

**asset valuation:** the value of a company based on the total worth of its individual assets minus liabilities.

**basket:** collection of indemnifications or insurance policies assigned a single dollar value and below which a seller is not responsible.

**book value:** net value of company assets as reported on the balance sheet. Book value of a share of stock equals equity (the total of common stock, paid-in capital and retained earnings) divided by the number of outstanding shares.

**boot:** any payment (e.g., cash or seller's notes) a buyer uses to supplement paying with all stock. While sellers do not pay taxes when receiving all stock, they may owe taxes on the boot received.

**business broker:** individual or company specializing in acquisition services, especially finding buyers for company sellers.

**business valuation expert:** see appraiser.

**C Corporation:** an ordinary corporation that pays taxes, limits the liability of its shareholders and acts as a legal entity.

**ceiling:** maximum amount a seller agrees to reimburse a buyer for certain liabilities after a sale.

**closing:** transfer of a company from seller to buyer by exchanging asset titles or stock certificates, and cash, stock or notes.

**collar:** upper and lower limit on the price of stock used to pay a seller.

201

**comfort letter:** opinion written by a CPA for buyer on financial condition since the last audited statements.

**confidentiality agreement (aka nondisclosure agreement):** buyer promises not to reveal confidential information about a selling company prior to closing.

**contingency fee:** fee to outsiders (e.g., investment bankers) for services in executing a sale and dependent on the purchase price.

**convertible debentures:** notes a seller accepts in a purchase price that can be exchanged at some future date for a fixed amount of buyer stock.

**convertible preferred stock:** buyer stock more secure than common stock that can be exchanged at some future date for a fixed number of shares of common stock.

**current ratio:** an expression of company liquidity determined by dividing current assets by current liabilities.

**debentures:** notes not backed by any specific property.

**discounted future cash flow:** see present value method.

**discount rate:** percentage representing future interest and used to obtain present value of future cash flow.

**due diligence:** thorough investigation and examination of a company.

**earn-out:** an agreement whereby a seller earns part of the purchase price or bonus out of company profit.

**employment contract:** agreement committing a seller to work for a buyer in the acquired company.

**engagement letter:** agreement between selling company and advisor's banker for services in selling the company.

**equity:** net worth of a company; common equity is the same thing as common stock.

**escrow account:** portion of purchase price set aside to pay for claims by a buyer against a former owner.

**exclusive agency agreement:** seller agreement with business broker promising exclusive right to represent the seller in finding a buyer and to receive a commission from a sale to any buyer except if the seller locates the buyer.

**exclusive agreement:** seller agreement with business broker promising exclusive right to represent the seller in finding a buyer and to receive a commission from a sale to any buyer.

**fairness opinion:** opinion by investment banker or other business valuation expert for shareholders of selling company affirming the fairness of a proposed purchase price.

**financials:** financial statements of a company, including balance sheet, income statement and statement of retained earnings.

**finder:** individual or company specializing in locating buyers for sellers.

**going business value:** see goodwill.

**going concern:** characteristic of an active business with operations and finances that create value beyond company book assets.

**golden handcuffs:** condition imposed on a seller remaining with the acquired company that makes it very costly to leave.

**goodwill:** an intangible asset such as a company's earnings, growth, customer base or capable personnel, and assigned a value over and above the value of a company's equity. Usually associated with earnings potential in excess of "normal."

**Hart-Scott-Rodino Act:** federal antitrust act requiring buyer or seller to notify the Federal Trade Commission and U.S. Department of Justice of a pending sale, depending on the nature and size of the companies and the size of the transaction.

**indemnification:** guarantees against losses from statements of fact and conditions about a company should they later be found to be untrue or incorrect.

**installment sale:** deferral of payment of the purchase price and taxes on a sale. Purchase price is spread over two or more payments.

**intangible assets:** company's properties other than plant, equipment or fixtures. Includes goodwill, trademarks, patents, research, distribution networks, brand names and client lists.

**Lehman formula:** method for calculating fees for investment bankers assisting in a sale or merger and based on purchase price.

**letter of intent (aka memo of intent, memo of understanding, agreement in principle):** generally nonbinding agreement between buyer and seller on the broad terms of a sale and subject to later negotiation.

**leveraged buyout:** purchase of a company through various forms of debt that are paid off from the company's cash flow or sale of its assets.

**liquidation:** dissolution of a company by distributing all assets to stockholders, usually by selling all its assets and paying off liabilities.

**materiality:** legal principle applied to purchase agreements about the relative importance of statements of fact and conditions about a company.

**memo of intent:** see letter of intent.

**memo of understanding:** see letter of intent.

**merger (aka statutory merger):** legally combining two companies by the selling company transferring its assets to the buyer's books.

**mezzanine financing:** level of financing behind mortgage debt used in leveraged buyouts.

**net operating loss carryovers:** prior years' cumulative federal income tax losses that can reduce future taxes by offsetting future profits.

**net working capital:** total value of current, short-term assets (e.g., cash, receivables, inventory) minus current liabilities.

**no shopping clause:** agreement between seller and buyer that seller will not look for another buyer until negotiations are finished.

**non-balance sheet asset (or liability):** asset or liability that does not appear on the financials but has value or obligation and can influence purchase price (e.g., retiree health benefits).

**noncompete agreement:** promise by selling company executives not to engage in the same business as the buyer for a fixed number of years and in a specific geographical area.

**nondisclosure agreement:** see confidentiality agreement.

**nonraiding clause:** promise by seller not to hire former employees away from buyer's acquired company.

**normalizing:** recalculating profit-and-loss statement to show how profits could be increased by reducing select expenses.

**opinion letter:** see fairness opinion.

**partnership:** business owned by two or more people and not incorporated.

**passing:** see closing.

**performance bonus (aka success bonus, performance fee):** additional fee based on the sale price or a company's earnings. Refers either to fee paid to investment bankers at the successful completion of a sale or to a seller when an acquired company exceeds certain financial targets.

**piggyback:** method of registering stock with the Securities and Exchange Commission. Seller adds unregistered shares to a batch of shares a buyer is registering.

**pooling of interests:** accounting method used by buyers to combine the financial statements of buyer and seller.

**preferred stock:** class of stock that pays a fixed dividend and is more secure than common stock.

**present value method (aka discounted future cash flow):** method of valuing a company based on future earnings or cash flow that are restated in today's dollars.

**price/earnings ratio:** method of valuing a company by either the purchase price or price of stock as a multiple of earnings.

**pro forma:** hypothetical financial statement calculated to indicate various levels of past or future expenses and profits.

**promissory note:** paper promise for a certain amount of money to be paid in the future over a specified number of years and according to any other negotiated terms.

**purchase agreement:** legal, definitive agreement between buyer and seller setting forth the terms for the sale of a company.

**purchase method:** accounting method used by buyer to record acquisition of a company.

**quick ratio (aka asset test ratio):** Figure indicating company ability to pay off short-term debt. Calculated by adding cash, cash equivalents and current receivables, and dividing by current liabilities.

**registered stock:** company securities reviewed and filed with the Securities and Exchange Commission and available for public trading.

**representations and warranties:** statements of fact and guarantees about the condition of a company.

**restricted stock:** unregistered securities that cannot be traded publicly or that have other transfer restrictions on the certificate.

**retained earnings:** cumulative earnings recorded on the balance sheet kept by a company and not paid to shareholders as dividends.

**return on assets (aka return on investment):** figure used in valuing a company and calculated by dividing income by total assets or total assets less non-interest-bearing debt.

**return on equity:** figure used in valuing a company and calculated by dividing net income after taxes by equity.

**return on sales:** figure comparing a company's total sales to net income and a measure of how much a company is making on each sales dollar.

**sale bonus:** portion of purchase price that is an incentive for employees remaining with the acquired company.

**S Corporation:** IRS designation for a small corporation that offers the same limited liability as a C Corporation but generally does not pay taxes on the corporate level. Taxes on profits and losses are paid by individual shareholders.

**second-tier investment bankers:** acquisition specialists dealing in small and medium-sized companies.

**selling memorandum (aka selling document):** summary of company activities, products, finances and future prepared for potential buyers.

**shelf registration:** filing of securities with the Securities and Exchange Commission allowing their public sale on short notice.

**side letter:** written agreement between buyer and seller specified in a separate paper and not part of the purchase agreement.

**signing:** signing and agreeing to the terms of the purchase agreement. Not necessarily the actual transfer of a company.

**sole proprietorship:** an unincorporated business owned by an individual.

**solvency letter:** opinion from buyer's accountant affirming ability to pay off notes.

**statutory merger:** see merger.

**step-up:** basic accounting and/or tax function increasing the balance sheet value and tax basis of assets transferred from one company to another.

**stock swap:** sale of a company by buyer and seller exchanging stock in their companies.

**success bonus:** see performance bonus.

**survival:** how long a contract, warranty or indemnification remains in effect.

**Tax Reform Act:** sweeping change in tax law passed in 1986 that significantly altered the taxes applied to a sale or acquisition.

**transfer tax:** state tax imposed on the transfer of assets between companies.

**triangular merger:** in a company sale, seller and buyer each dissolve their corporations and create a third company to be controlled by the buyer.

**unregistered stock** (see also restricted stock): company securities used in a private offering and not eligible for public trading.

**valuation:** formal process of determining the worth of a company.

**warranties and representations:** see representations and warranties.

# SUGGESTED READING

Baumer, William Henry. *Buy, Sell, Merge: How To Do It.* Englewood Cliffs, New Jersey: Prentice-Hall, Inc., 1971.

Clark, John. *Business Merger and Acquisition Strategies.* Englewood Cliffs, New Jersey: Prentice-Hall, Inc., 1985.

Freund, James. *Anatomy of a Merger.* New York: Law Journal Press, 1976.

Goldstein, Arnold. *The Complete Guide to Buying and Selling a Business.* New York: Wiley, 1983.

Hartz, Peter. *Merger.* New York: Morrow, 1985.

Hopkins, Thomas. *Mergers, Acquisitions and Divestitures.* Homewood, Illinois: Dow Jones-Irwin, 1983.

Lovejoy, Frederick. *Buying, Merging and Selling a Business.* Princeton, New Jersey: F. Lovejoy Associates, 1968.

Marren, Joseph. *Mergers and Acquisitions.* Homewood, Illinois: Dow Jones-Irwin, 1985.

Morris, Joseph. *Acquisitions, Divestitures, Corporate Joint Ventures.* New York: Wiley, 1984.

Practicing Law Institute Course Handbook. *Acquiring or Selling the Privately Held Company.* New York, 1987.

Rubel, Stanley. *Guide to Selling a Business.* Chicago: Capital Publishing Corporation, 1977.

Scharf, Charles, Edward Shea, and George Beck. *Acquisitions, Mergers, Sales, Buyouts and Takeovers: A Handbook With Forms.* Englewood Cliffs, New Jersey: Prentice-Hall, Inc., Third Edition, 1985.

Sterling Publishing, *How to Buy and Sell a Small Business.* New York: Sterling Publishing, Inc., Revised edition, 1982.

# INDEX